You Can't, You Won't

A Life of Unarmed Combat

Gary Skyner
with Carol Fenlon

Matador
9 Priory Business Park,
Wistow Road, Kibworth Beauchamp,
Leicestershire. LE8 0RX
Tel: 0116 279 2299
Email: books@troubador.co.uk
Web: www.troubador.co.uk/matador
Twitter: @matadorbooks

ISBN 978 1785898 631

British Library Cataloguing in Publication Data.
A catalogue record for this book is available from the British Library.

Printed and bound by CPI Group (UK) Ltd, Croydon, CR0 4YY
Typeset in 11pt Aldine401 BT by Troubador Publishing Ltd, Leicester, UK

Matador is an imprint of Troubador Publishing Ltd

For my mother
Frances Skyner
You gave me life… You gave me everything.

Acknowledgements

I am indebted to Deborah Jack, director of the Thalidomide Trust, for helpful comments on the manuscript, and to *Private Eye* magazine, Trinity Mirror plc newspapers and the *Daily Express* for their kind permission to reproduce pages from their publications.

Contents

Foreword   xi

1 'He'll Never Amount to Much'   1

2 A Most Suitable Drug for Pregnant Women   8

3 'Your Child Is a Thalidomide Baby'   16

4 David and Goliath   35

5 Goals and Goalposts   58

6 The Grand National of Life   70

7 A Funny Thing Happened to Me…   94

8 Giant Steps   113

9 Pissing in the Wind   134

10 That's Showbiz   149

11 After 9/11   168

12 'You Could Do With Losing a Bit of Weight'   185

13 Dark Days   205

14 Changing the World   210

15 Losing My Rock   218

16 Still Smouldering After All These Years   230

17 The Special Ones   241

References   246

FOREWORD
by Ricky Tomlinson

I first met Gary Skyner in 1987 when he was just starting out in stand-up comedy. We were both on the same bill and though he was new to the game, I was impressed by his talent and his tenacity. Later I ran into him now and then on the circuit, especially with us both being Scousers, and gradually we became friends.

Those first impressions stayed with me and grew stronger as I got to know Gary better. In my career I've met so many celebrities, stars of stage and screen and sporting personalities, all determined to be top of their game, but I've never met anyone as courageous as Gary.

Entertainment is a hard business. It takes 100% effort. For Gary it takes twice that. In that sense he's an inspiration to others round him. He's worked with me many times and never let me down, despite his disability. I think that disability has held him back in his career, especially where television work is concerned, but Gary always bounces back from disappointments. Despite his many successes Gary loves to achieve, and I know he won't give up until they are shovelling dirt on top of him. I wish him the great future he deserves.

I think this book should be read especially by people with

any disability to give them the inspiration that they need to achieve heights they never thought possible, which is what my mate Gary Skyner has done.

Ricky Tomlinson

Chapter 1

'He'll Never Amount to Much'

The night I was born there were fireworks, literally. It was 5 November 1959, and across Liverpool bonfires were being lit. The year 1959 itself was an amazing year, with Britain finally putting the dark days of post-World War II austerity behind her and looking forward to the sunny, sultry promise of the 1960s.

Worldwide it was a period of change with revolution in Cuba, poor relations between America and Russia, fears of Communist takeovers and the threat of nuclear war, but for most Britons things looked rosy. Nationalisation and the developing welfare state were stabilising the conditions of the working classes, there was almost full employment and a wealth of new consumer goods were coming on to the market for people to buy. The newly elected Conservative government swept to power under Harold Macmillan and the slogan *You've never had it so good*.

None of this would have particularly concerned my mother Frances on this day, as she lay in Sefton General Hospital's maternity wing struggling to give birth to her first child. However, she must have caught some of the nation's celebratory mood as she pushed me out to the accompaniment of rockets and bangers outside. Birth is a painful but joyous occasion, so I am told: a hard labour rewarded by the long-awaited perfect baby. But my mother's joy was short-lived. Even as she was flooded with relief on hearing my first cry someone muttered,

'It's a pity,' and I was whisked away before she could see me. The question every mother asks,

'Is he all right?' was left hanging in the empty air as she was left alone in growing terror.

My father, Brian Skyner, had rushed to the hospital arriving at twenty past six, shortly after I was born. Rain was dampening the bonfires but had failed to affect his anticipation as he waited in the ward's reception area. His spirits soared when the ward sister came to him and, in answer to his eager question, informed him that Frances had given birth to a boy. However, his happiness died when he saw the solemn demeanour of the doctor, who then entered the room. His heart sank as the medic's clipped words dropped cold stones in his mind.

'I'm afraid your son has been born with foreshortened upper limbs,' the doctor said.

The doctor, taking refuge in detachment, went on to describe my condition. Although otherwise apparently healthy I had no thumbs, webbing to three fingers and – as far as they could tell before an X-ray – lacked some bones in my arms and shoulders. This clinical description did not prepare my father for the sight of me. When my blanket was unwrapped, revealing the two flipper-like appendages that would serve me for arms, he could not help recoiling. The nurse in the room said,

'It would be better if God had taken him,' and my father responded,

'Yes, it would.' Not an auspicious entry into the world.

Reeling with shock, my father then had to try to comfort my mother, who still hadn't seen me and who was unaware of the true extent of my deformities. She was not to see me for another two days. Nowadays this wouldn't happen. Awareness of the window of opportunity for maternal bonding is strong now, but back in the 1950s babies were often brought up under strict regimes of discipline to instil regular routines and avoid spoiling. Childcare books recommended only picking up your baby at regular times for feeding, and not giving in to crying children with cuddles. Furthermore, attitudes to disability were not what they are today. Many children with physical and/or mental disabilities were hidden away in homes and special schools. It would be many years before inclusive policies towards disability were implemented, and even now there are still many problems surrounding living in our society with a disability of any kind.

Fortunately for me, my parents were enlightened in this respect, and determined that I should live as normal a life as possible. But more of that later.

Other thalidomiders were not so lucky. In her autobiography, Louise Medus (née Mason) describes how she was taken to a residential institution straight from hospital and her mother did not see her until she was five weeks old. Twenty-two other thalidomide children were already living at this care home when she arrived there (Medus & Swain, 2012).

I don't know if pressure was put on my parents to have me put into care. Certainly comments made by the hospital staff might suggest so. The attending doctor told my father,

'Poor mite. If he survives he'll never amount to much.'

However, knowing my mum, I believe she would never even have considered giving me up. I'm not so sure about my dad. I think he saw my deformity as a slur on his manhood – maybe something he would want to hide from sight. I also know that at that time health professionals were encouraged to persuade parents of disabled children to put them into care.

Luckily, not everyone took such a negative view. One kindly Jamaican nurse told my mum,

'God has chosen you to have this particular child because he trusts you will love and cherish him forever.' (Skyner & Sampson, 2006, p. 21.)

I'm sure that even if my father had listened to the doctors, who were writing me off as a hopeless case, my mother would have overruled him. She would have argued that as a couple they were responsible for me, and that they needed to stick together and bring me up as best they could. That is how my mum was. Thankfully she was always proactive on my behalf, encouraging and empowering me to lead as normal a life as possible, whereas my dad always seemed to veto things and try to keep me safely indoors.

Louise Medus claims in her book that the lack of bonding experience with her mother at birth, and in those early weeks, resulted in permanent damage to their relationship.

Did I miss that first bonding experience immediately after birth? Obviously I have no memory of how I felt, left alone in my crib surrounded by pity, horror and negativity and without the reassuring nearness of my mother after nine months of living in her warmth. I only know that two days after my birth, when I was put into my mother's arms, a dialogue of love began immediately… a dialogue that was only checked by her death in 2012.

★

I went home with my parents ten days after my birth and was christened Gary Brian Skyner on Sunday 13 December at St Clement's Church in Toxteth Park. Perhaps I cried when the water from the font was poured on my head.

There were many more tears ahead for my parents. Neither they nor anyone else at that stage had any idea what had caused the damage I had suffered. Naturally they blamed themselves. The doctors had told them it was probably something to do with their genetic make-up but, while they must have reassured them that it was no fault of their own and was possibly a throwback from earlier generations, my family thought differently. While my father secretly blamed himself for having some defect to his manhood my mother's side of the family knew otherwise. They agreed the damage was down to earlier generations, but they believed it was because there was a gipsy curse on the family.

Many years earlier a curse had been laid on Mum's mum, Catherine Ellis, by a gipsy who predicted she would never have grandchildren. The curse had seemed to come true, as my mum's brother and three sisters had all married before her but no grandchildren had arrived.

So you can imagine the family's excitement when my mum broke the news that she was pregnant. All their hopes were riding on her having a successful delivery, only to be dashed when my dad broke the news about my deformity.

'It's the gipsy curse,' Catherine Ellis screamed immediately.

For those first few days my dad didn't allow anyone except both sets of grandparents to visit the hospital, so that he and my mum would have some time to recover from the shock of my birth and get used to me. So it was not until after I came home that I was really introduced to the rest of the family.

The family I was born into was a traditional working-class family from one of those tight-knit communities that were destined to disintegrate under the social reorganisation of the 1960s. Soon inner cities would be transformed, and generations of social relationships broken up and scattered to overspill estates and new towns.

The Lodge Lane area of Toxteth where my family lived was then a mostly white community, where everyone knew each other. Later it would become a mixed-race area, but in the late 1950s it was still home to traditional working-class families.

Both my mum's parents and my dad's parents were brought up in the area. My mum's parents lived in Camp Street, where she was brought up, and her dad worked at the water board in nearby Beaumont Street.

My mum had four sisters and a brother, so her mum had her hands full without going out to work. My dad's dad, Albert, who we always called 'Pa', was a school caretaker. My Grandma Skyner worked at Watson's car showroom in Birkenhead, cleaning big cars and limousines. Everybody worked in those days, and there was virtually no unemployment.

Mum and Dad on their wedding day

My mum and dad both had white-collar occupations. My mum was a nurse, working at the Meccano factory in Binns Road, off Edge Lane. Her sister Edie also worked there in the assembly room, making Dinky toys. My dad was a civil servant in the employment service but before marriage he did two years' national service in the RAF. When I was born he was working at the Liverpool labour exchange in Renshaw Street.

Theirs seems to have been a real love relationship, although they met on a blind date. They married on Valentine's Day 1959 and my mum fell pregnant with me almost immediately. Apparently it was a normal pregnancy, but at some point during the second and third months Mum's doctor prescribed a new drug called Distaval to combat her morning sickness.

Distaval was the brand name under which thalidomide was marketed in the UK.

Chapter 2

A Most Suitable Drug for Pregnant Women

Chemie Grünenthal is a name that has haunted me all my adult life, since I was old enough to understand what happened to me and my family.

Many people think of the thalidomide disaster as a tragic accident: something unforeseeable that happened to a reputable drug company, a company that still holds its head high in the pharmaceutical industry today.

It may all seem a long time ago; water under the bridge; another world, where safety procedures were less robust than they are now. Anyway, didn't the companies involved pay compensation to the victims? It's a sad story but lessons were learnt… and perhaps it's time to put it all behind us and move on, isn't it?

Well, I and others like me can't move on. I've had to live with it all my life, and although I lead a fuller life than many people do – and I've never wasted time feeling sorry for myself – there can be no resolution, reconciliation or forgiveness in my heart until Chemie Grünenthal stands up and admits what it has done.

This company wriggled out of a prosecution for intent to commit bodily harm (note the word *intent*) and involuntary manslaughter. It has steadfastly refused to accept responsibility or admit liability for killing thousands of babies worldwide and maiming thousands more. The surviving thalidomiders only received an apology for the tragedy from the firm in 2012, fifty-six years after the first thalidomide child was born.

When I think about Chemie Grünenthal I get angry, and by the time you get to the end of this chapter I hope you will understand why. The only thing that would give me some peace of mind would be for the company to admit what it did and to show some compassion for the remaining survivors by ensuring they are properly taken care of for the years they have left. It's not a personal thing. I'm well aware that the original perpetrators (who were never called to justice) are long gone, but as a company Chemie Grünenthal still holds the primary responsibility for creating thalidomide and marketing it to a world that trusted in the integrity of scientists. And, if you think it couldn't happen again, perhaps you will have changed your mind after you have read this book.

*

In the 1950s the new German Federal Republic was rising from the ashes of its Second World War defeat and, perhaps more importantly, struggling to rebuild its shattered image in the eyes of the world. One area in which it excelled was its pharmaceutical industry. During the war German scientists had been given carte blanche for medical and chemical research, much of it conducted to aid the war effort and the glorious new world vision of the Third Reich. Current research suggests they were able to use the facilities offered by the Third Reich's infamous prisoner of war camps and concentration camps with their ready supply of guinea pigs. As a result German companies had a leading edge in the post-war development of medicine and pharmaceuticals.

I wasn't born till 1959, but the 1950s must have been

the strangest of times. World War II drew a line, after which nothing would ever be the same again. The horror of it would be put away, never to happen again. Its physical scars, bombed-out cities and ruined lives would be erased and replaced with shining new towns and city centres. It would be a brave new world with full employment, good wages and homes fit for heroes. A breath of fresh air blew through Europe as national economies boomed. New inventions to make life easier and more colourful flooded on to the market, promising to banish the dullness of post-war austerity for good.

But in life it seems that there is a good and a bad side to everything. Along with the general air of excitement that characterised the late 1950s came new fears. As technology speeded up the older, slower way of life was lost, and instead became a rat race where you had to vie for promotion and more money in order to keep up with the lifestyle of this new consumer world. *Make do and mend* turned to *Go out and buy the latest*. And you were so much more aware of this because of that other new thing, the eye in the corner of your new lounge: the wonder of television. It kept you up to date with what you should be wearing and what you needed to get for your home and family. Even more significantly, it kept you informed about all the frightening things going on in the rest of the world… over which you had no control whatsoever.

Only people who lived through the 1950s and 1960s will remember the absolute terror of nuclear war that prevailed in that period with the memories of Hiroshima and Nagasaki still fresh in the collective mind, and the intimidating cold war stand-off between Russia and the USA. Germany had been defeated, only to be replaced by more superpowers locked in a seemingly endless conflict in which Europe had little power to intervene. A fear of the mushroom cloud hung over everyone.

It was small wonder that people increasingly turned to chemical means to give them respite. Some turned to alcohol, others to drugs. The drugs manufacturers (like the rest of industry) had boomed, and new drugs were produced and aggressively marketed to a public hungry for easy solutions to their ills. The two major areas of post-war research were antibiotics and sedatives. Barbiturate sedatives had been developed and were now the order of the day to calm frazzled nerves and soothe away anxieties, but overdosing was a common problem. People were using them to commit suicide, which did not bode well for the producers' marketing strategies. The hunt was on for a less toxic sedative: something that would satisfy the pill-popping public's demand for a 'little helper' without putting them in any danger. In 1956 Chemie Grünenthal announced that they had found it.

The company was formed in 1946, and it was at first a relatively small firm operating from a disused copper foundry in the village of Stolburg, near Aachen. It was a subsidiary of a cosmetics company which produced fairly run-of-the-mill ointments, cough mixtures, disinfectants and herbal remedies. It was an innocuous beginning, but a closer look at the company's staff structure already sets alarm bells ringing.

Dr Heinrich Mückter, the appointed director of Chemie Grünenthal's research and development team, had been a staunch member of the Nazi party and the former medical officer to the Superior Command of the German occupation forces based in Krakow, Poland. What kind of medical work Mückter was engaged in during this period is lost in the mists of history but Sir Harold Evans, writing in The *Guardian* (14 November 2014), claims he experimented on prisoners in Polish labour camps in an attempt to find a typhus vaccine, and that many of the subjects of his experiments died. Mückter was sought by the Polish authorities after the war, but escaped arrest.

Hermann Wirtz, a partner of the original cosmetics firm and an appointed director of the new company, was also a former member of the Nazi party. Perhaps this was unremarkable at that time, when many German citizens would be doing their best to live down their former status. However, it makes me wonder if Wirtz still held to his old values in engaging Mückter – who, by all accounts, was the archetypal Nazi, a man of chilling and arrogant appearance (Brynner and Stephens, 2001). Another Grünenthal employee, Dr Martin Staemmler, had been involved in the racial hygiene and eugenics programmes so beloved of the Nazis. Even more sinister was the fact that Otto Ambros, the non-executive chairman of the company, had been sentenced to eight years' imprisonment at the Nuremberg war trials for his role in the construction of the Auschwitz IG Farben plant because he was one of the inventors of the nerve gas sarin. Ambros had been given early release to assist the US army chemical corps before joining Grünenthal (Evans, ibid.).

It beggars belief that these people – who had spent much of their lives soaking up the propaganda of the Third Reich and participating freely in its doctrines, and who were accustomed to experimenting with and destroying human life without compunction – should now be admitted to positions of responsibility and trust in any medical concern. However, this was post-war Germany and who in that nation did not feel some responsibility for things done in the name of the Third Reich, even if their only part had been to close their eyes and their minds to what went on? Germans wanted to forgive themselves and put the past behind them. And anyway... the ex-Nazi scientists were now working for healing, for the good of mankind, weren't they?

This was an over-optimistic view. Under Mückter's directorship it wasn't long before ominous signs appeared. In its early days Chemie Grünenthal was engaged in developing new antibiotics which, at the time, were the wonder solution to humanity's illnesses. Mückter succeeded in developing penicillin from moulds and the company enjoyed some success from this, securing lucrative government contracts and expanding its workforce and operations. However, every other pharmaceutical manufacturer was working on antibiotics so that the market rapidly flooded, and any new drug needed some exceptional quality to secure a share. In 1952, 1953 and 1954 Mückter produced three new drugs for which he made extravagant claims, which were later discredited. It also appeared that he rushed these drugs on to the market without first rigorously testing them. Although such a practice was not unknown among other pharmaceutical companies in the race for commercial success it showed a repeated disregard for safety, which would be a crucial factor in the thalidomide disaster in the case of Chemie Grünenthal.

While continuing to experiment with antibiotics Mückter had an eye on the developing market in sedatives. Ex-army sergeant Wilhelm Kunz had been recruited as head of research, and Dr Herbert Keller had been engaged to head up pharmacological testing. It was while Kunz was attempting to develop antibiotics from peptides that he created the compound that would become thalidomide. Although the team had no specific purpose for the compound, they patented it after creating it. They then began animal testing to see what it might be used for.

What they discovered was that no matter how high a dose of the compound was administered no toxic effects were observed, so they then reasoned that if the drug proved to have sedative qualities it would capture the market as a safe alternative to barbiturates. Whether thalidomide ever demonstrated sedative qualities is debatable, by all accounts, but the Chemie Grünenthal team began clinical trials on humans for sedative effects.

Careful testing at this point would have at least revealed thalidomide's most common side effect, which is that of causing peripheral neuritis (damage to the nerve endings). And testing on pregnant women would have limited the teratogenic (deforming) effects on unborn children to a small number instead of the epidemic that was to come. However, Mückter was in a hurry. Competition was fierce in the industry, and he wanted to be first on the market with his wonder drug. Additionally, both he and Kunz were entitled to a percentage of any profits made from drugs they produced, so it was in their personal interests to get thalidomide to market as soon as possible.

Consequently, instead of conducting controlled tests, drug samples were randomly given out to GPs and some Grünenthal employees, often without any proper records or follow-up. Again, it makes me wonder how anyone would consider this to be acceptable practice. Could it be that an ingrained belief in the old methods of Nazi experimentation explains such carelessness and lack of concern for human safety? In any case, insufficient time was allowed for any results to come back and be collated before rushing the drug on to the market.

Thalidomide was officially released in Germany on 1 October 1957 under the brand name Contergan. The accompanying literature and advertisements emphasised the total safety of the drug for old and young alike and its suitability for a number of conditions, as well as sleeplessness. In Germany it was available over the counter without prescription, so there was no record of who was buying the drug or for what condition.

Aggressive marketing by Chemie Grünenthal soon resulted in thalidomide being available in thirty-seven countries under a variety of brand names. In 1958 Distillers Company (Biochemicals) Ltd, (DCBL), a branch of the huge Distillers drinks firm, secured a contract to manufacture and distribute thalidomide in Great Britain and the Commonwealth countries under the trade name Distaval. Under the terms of the contract DCBL were obliged to begin marketing the drug within nine months of signing. This did not allow them time to conduct proper clinical trials of their own so they happily accepted Chemie Grünenthal's assurances that the drug was completely safe, even adding to their own labelling the information given out by the German manufacturer that thalidomide was *a most suitable drug for pregnant women and nursing mothers.*

Left: Dr Heinrich Mückter. Right: Otto Ambros pictured at the time of the Nuremburg war trials.

Chapter 3

'Your Child Is a Thalidomide Baby'

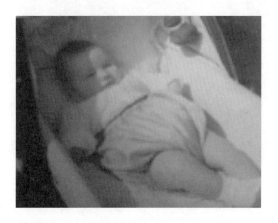

I was one of the first thalidomide babies to be born in the UK, but of course I knew nothing about that. My first memory is of lying in my pram and looking at the doors of the houses along our street, which were all painted the same shade of green by the council. My parents lived with my father's parents in a small terraced house in Aspen Grove, just round the corner from my mum's parents. My mum said she was happy there in those first few years of marriage, despite the problems caused by my birth. She spoke of being 'so in love' (Skyner & Sampson, ibid., p. 23), and paid tribute to the support she got from my dad's parents as well as from her own.

The early 1960s in Britain were years of exciting prospects as the nation approached a period of affluence unknown since the war, with an accompanying explosion of technology and culture. I was surrounded by love from the whole community. Within the extended family I was the first grandchild, and I was fussed over and petted. There was no shortage of offers to babysit while my parents enjoyed the occasional night out, drinking and dancing in Liverpool's burgeoning nightlife.

Albert and Alice Skyner, my paternal grandparents. My parents lived with them during my early childhood... lots of happy memories.

Although Mum's memories of my early years were happy ones – memories of a family full of love and of romance in her still-new married relationship – there were dark spots, with the occasional passer-by making cruel and thoughtless comments. On one occasion an old lady, on seeing me in my pram, asked my mother if my condition was a result of an attempted abortion. You can imagine how that made her feel.

Another dark shadow was cast by my Grandmother Ellis's belief in the power of the gipsy curse. No one knows how the curse came about or what my gran did to deserve it. Grandma Ellis was quite meek and mild regarding dealing with hawkers compared to Grandma Skyner, who couldn't abide them.

There were a lot of door-to-door callers in those days, and when one knocked at my Grandma Skyner's door all the kids in the street would gather to watch the entertainment.

'Buy a lucky charm from me,' the hawker would demand, and my gran would say,

'Just wait a minute while I get my purse.' All the kids would be waiting, giggling with expectation, as she returned with a bucket of water, chucked it over the hapless hawker and shouted, 'Now clear off!'

I wouldn't have been surprised if she had been cursed a few times, but it was my other nan who suffered, and suffered badly, for taking it seriously. Since my birth she must have brooded on my condition and blamed herself for bringing the curse on the family, because six months after I was born she attempted suicide by slashing her wrists. This made my mother feel guilty and take blame on herself for my condition, and for bringing pain to the rest of the family. Fortunately she was able to discuss her feelings with staff at Alder Hey Children's Hospital, where I had to make regular visits. They were able to dispel the negative thoughts and encouraged her and my father to try for another child as soon as they felt ready.

She and my father discussed this and agreed to try for another baby, but felt they should wait until life had settled down and they had established a settled routine with me. They also felt they should wait until my Grandma Ellis had recovered from her injuries and was in a better state of mind. It would be another two and a half years before my sister Karen was born, by which time I was growing fast and becoming aware of the world around me.

I was pampered as a baby and as a small child and I don't recall having any fear of anything, although my father was always a stern presence in my life. When I was very small Mr Allen, who kept a shop on Lodge Lane, would give my mum a toy or a Dinky car for me every time she went by with the pram. My Aunty Edie, who worked at the Meccano factory, would also bring home Dinky toys for me, so I amassed a huge collection. If only I had kept them.

I must have soon become aware that I was physically different from other people but I was never made to feel different, except that everyone fussed over me – which I suppose I took for granted. It wasn't all a bed of roses, though. In those early years my mum had to take me to Alder Hey Children's Hospital every other week. I was fitted with leather arm splints which needed regular readjustments as I grew bigger. These rubbed and often caused sores – but fortunately I had surgery later to implant plastic bones in my arms and to separate my fingers, so I didn't need prosthetics. My legs are short but normal so I didn't have many problems learning to walk, although my shortened arms made balance difficult and if I fell I was unable to save myself from injury. Thankfully I was spared the indignity of some of the contraptions invented to help other thalidomide children as aids to walking, and to looking after themselves.

Prosthetic development was then in its infancy, and artificial arms and legs were clumsy and difficult to manoeuvre. They were also extremely heavy for a small child with undeveloped muscles to deal with. Artificial arms were powered by gas canisters that were strapped to children's backs and hissed with every movement, making their owners look more like urban spacemen than ordinary people. Most of the kids hated prosthetics and eventually abandoned them, getting around as best they could with what nature (or rather thalidomide) had given them. I'm the same. I wouldn't thank you now for the best artificial arms in the world. I'm comfortable with what I have and I manage pretty well. But then, I'm one of the luckier ones. I do have legs and arms and hands of a sort.

Artificial limbs made for a thalidomide child in the 1960s by the DHSS Limb Fitting Centre in Roehampton, London.

I had many operations in my first thirteen years. I spent a lot of time as an inpatient at Alder Hey Children's Hospital in Liverpool and also at Whiston Hospital, often for weeks at a time, so I soon got used to the hospital environment. I think the longest continuous time I was in was eight weeks. When I came out there would also be regular check-ups and physio appointments. Of course, operations were painful and frightening for a small child and the couple of days I would spend in hospital being prepared for surgery would be scary, but I knew that once it was over I would be petted and spoilt by the family and I would be able to play with the toys and the other children on the ward. That was quite a fun experience that I looked forward to, despite the pain of the operation.

I didn't get many chances to mix with other children when I was very small. My sister Karen was born when I was two and a half on 30 January 1962, but she never got the attention that I did. Although the whole family was delighted at the birth of a perfect baby, thus dispelling for good the gipsy curse, I was always the focus of attention for friends and family. It is a sad fact that the thalidomide tragedy affected not only the immediate victims but rippled outwards to change the lives of siblings and extended family as well, a fact never taken into consideration in calculating compensation.

I remember that, as she grew, Karen would rock back and forward on her chair in what I now realise may have been a symptom of psychological distress. But I was happy in my little world, cocooned in the loving atmosphere of my family. However, all that was about to change when I started going to school. Before that day came along, however, something else happened that rocked my family to the core.

My mother had called out the family doctor, suspecting that my sister Karen was suffering from chickenpox. The attending physician was a German locum. On noticing my disability he asked my mum what had happened to me, and when she said I was born that way he asked if she had taken any medication during her pregnancy. My mum rummaged in the kitchen cupboard and produced a medicine bottle containing one tablet of Distaval. The doctor told her, to her astonishment,

'Your child is a thalidomide baby.'

He went on to explain that a charitable trust was being set up in London to help such children, and told her to get in touch with it. My mum barely listened to this talk of help and compensation because she was utterly traumatised by the thought that she had taken something that had caused my terrible condition. In her mind the fault was all hers for being weak enough to take medication, and it was a long time before she could truly rid herself of this guilt. The news seemed to come as a partial relief to my father, however, who now knew there was definitely no genetic failure on his part. This fear had lingered in his mind, even though Karen was a perfectly normal healthy baby.

By this time the tragic consequences of putting thalidomide on the market had come to light. Mention thalidomide and most people think of birth defects, probably because these are the most shockingly visible side effects of the drug. But in fact another side effect, peripheral neuritis, was the first to become evident. This was probably more widespread than the phocomelia (literally seal-like or flipper-like deformity of the limbs) with which it is usually associated.

Although the first thalidomide child was born without ears in 1956 to a Grünenthal employee (who had been given free samples of thalidomide), it was reports of peripheral neuritis in patients taking the drug that first raised the alarm in the medical community. Peripheral neuritis affects the extremities, manifesting in tingling and numbness due to nerve damage. If left untreated it progresses to loss of feeling and function in the limbs, and in many cases the damage is irreversible.

Lesser side effects of dizziness and nausea had been reported even before thalidomide was released, but Chemie Grünenthal ignored these complaints. However, when a number of doctors began claiming an association between thalidomide and peripheral neuritis in 1959 the company was forced to respond. But it only did so by issuing written denials that Contergan was responsible, and also by denying that they had received reports of neuritis from other physicians. This action did not stem the tide of complaints, and by 1960 academic papers had begun to appear in the medical press linking thalidomide to cases of peripheral neuritis.

Peripheral neuritis takes some time to manifest, and its association with thalidomide only occurred in patients who had been taking the drug over a long period of time. Thalidomide had been on sale for nearly three years in many countries across the world, but by the time the medical world woke up to the association between pregnant women taking it and birth defects the response was merely to recommend that thalidomide should only be available on prescription (rather than asking for a complete ban pending further testing).

Unbelievably, thalidomide had been on sale in Germany and in some other countries as an over-the-counter remedy for self-medication in several forms and mixtures that catered to a wide variety of medical problems. Perhaps the most horrifying of these was a liquid form called Contergan Saft, promoted as a safe sedative for crying babies. In Sweden this was even marketed under a name which meant 'babysitter' (The *Sunday Times* Insight Team, 1979). Despite increasing reports of side effects Chemie Grünenthal continued to market thalidomide as a safe, non-toxic cure-all, so safe that it could even be given to babies without ill effects.

Initially, sales of thalidomide were huge. In the first year of marketing Chemie Grünenthal was selling 90,000 packets a month. By 1960, faced with increasing unrest regarding the efficacy of their wonder drug, the company set about seeking favourable reports to silence their critics rather than initiating research into what was actually happening to patients who had taken the drug.

The critical voices grew louder, but Chemie Grünenthal's response was to attempt to defuse the situation by saying that sales of thalidomide were so high that it was inevitable that a few cases of adverse reactions would occur. In a letter to

DCBL, the British distributors of thalidomide under the trade name Distaval, Dr Mückter claimed that, in the rare event of reaction, symptoms would disappear on ceasing to take the drug. This statement was not based on any clinical research, and proved to be patently untrue. From this we can see that Mückter, as an official representative of Chemie Grünenthal, not only showed no care or compassion for the consumers on whom his livelihood depended but was prepared to lie blatantly to protect his own and the company's interests.

It was not until August 1961, following a barrage of medical criticism by respected and knowledgeable physicians, that Chemie Grünenthal capitulated and applied for thalidomide to be placed on prescription-only status. Even then this only took place in parts of Germany, leaving the drug on sale to all and sundry in many other areas and countries. However, the firm's sales were falling rapidly. They were facing many lawsuits from patients suffering from peripheral neuritis, and even their own executives were beginning to doubt the value of their wonder drug. Who knows how many patients actually suffered the devastating effects of peripheral neuritis? Estimates vary between 4,000 and 40,000 in West Germany alone (the *Sunday Times* Insight Team, ibid.).

Chemie Grünenthal certainly appears as the villain of the piece in this unfolding tragedy. But the companies who accepted their sales pitches and rushed to obtain agreements to sell thalidomide in their own countries, no doubt with an eye to the fat profits to be made, are also accountable.

In Britain thalidomide went to market in April 1958, with a sales campaign that stressed the safety of the drug despite the fact that DCBL had not completed clinical trials before releasing Distaval but had just accepted Chemie Grünenthal's assurances. It is horrifying to note that in 1961, when surely complaints about thalidomide in internationally read scientific journals such as the *British Medical Journal* should have been seen by DCBL's pharmacological team, the company issued a promotional leaflet recommending the use of thalidomide for a wide variety of conditions including neurology, psychology, *paediatrics and obstetrics*, (The *Sunday Times* Insight Team, ibid.).

Such leaflets made it sound as if the makers of thalidomide were fully aware of how the drug functioned and had actually conducted tests involving the relevant patient groups, when in fact no such knowledge existed. The manner of thalidomide's action in the human body was at that time unknown and would remain so for many years, and neither Chemie Grünenthal nor DCBL knew whether thalidomide had any effect on pregnant women. If they had tested to find out, I and many others would have been spared a lifetime of struggle.

As in Germany, occurrences of peripheral neuritis were being linked to thalidomide, and one of DCBL's own pharmacologists reported toxic results when thalidomide in a liquid form was tested on animals. Apparently the liquid form was more easily absorbed by the body, allowing the true toxic properties of the drug to wreak havoc. Despite these findings, incredibly DCBL went ahead with marketing a liquid form of thalidomide, stating in its advertising material that it was particularly suitable for children (The *Sunday Times* Insight Team, 1979). Later it would be revealed that similar results had been obtained in the USA when Richardson-Merrell had tested a syrup form on rats. The mixture killed the majority of subjects it was administered to. Just like DCBL, Richardson-Merrell did not report these findings, and went ahead with their plans to market the drug (Brynner and Stephens, 2001).

In Britain, faced with a rash of complaints about side effects, the sensible thing for Distillers to have done was to withdraw Distaval pending further research. Instead they simply reworded their leaflets to emphasise low toxicity rather than no toxicity while still touting its suitability for all age groups, including pregnant women. They also included a statement that, in the unlikely event of the patient developing peripheral neuritis, promptly discontinuing the drug would cause the neuritis to disappear.

At this point thalidomide's most tragic side effect had still not been discovered, despite the fact that thousands of deformed babies had already been born in the four years since it went on sale. Remember, thalidomide was on sale in thirty-seven countries. DCBL's licence covered not only the British Isles but all the Commonwealth countries, including Australia and Canada. Communist countries with closed economies such as China and the USSR were fortunate in that they were safe from being drawn into the tragedy. The USA was a different matter, however, and Chemie Grünenthal was keen to exploit this enormous market. The US pharmaceutical company Richardson-Merrell was persuaded to apply for a licence to distribute thalidomide under the brand name Kevadon in October 1958.

Richardson-Merrell was part of the Vicks company, which was well known for Vicks VapoRub (a decongestant). The company planned to begin selling Kevadon in March 1961, and had 10 million tablets ready to release on to the US market. At the same time they planned to market a drug to lower cholesterol known as MER/29. It was later proved that MER/29 had caused cataracts and other side effects in tests on monkeys, and that Richardson-Merrell had covered this up when reporting their clinical findings to the Federal Drug Agency (FDA). As a result they received an $80,000 fine, and were forced to pay around $200 million in compensation to patients who had been damaged by MER/29.

I have already noted how Richardson-Merrell covered up findings of toxicity in tests of thalidomide syrup. As they had already made their application for licence to the FDA before these tests were done they simply failed to report them. It's clear that the behaviour of Chemie Grünenthal in making false claims and covering up evidence was not an isolated incident. DCBL in Britain was happy to make claims that had no backup evidence or foundation in existing knowledge, and Richardson-Merrell in the US showed a similar lack of concern for its consumer groups. To me this means that the catastrophe of thalidomide is not just a result of the callous Nazi mentality of a few individuals, but it exists in the greed for and the worship of profit demonstrated by capitalist concerns worldwide. It is this demonstration of global culpability that makes me strong in my pursuit of these companies, even today. The original individuals responsible are long gone, but these companies still bear responsibility through their corporate aims and methods.

Fortunately for the USA Dr Frances Kelsey, the FDA medical officer assigned to review Richardson-Merrell's application to market Kevadon, spotted many inadequacies in their application and refused to grant them a licence. A long-drawn-out process of submission and resubmission ensued, with Kelsey finding more unsatisfactory information at each stage. Then the European reports of peripheral neuritis in the medical press came to her attention, causing her to ask for even more stringent evidence regarding the safety of Kevadon.

The deadline Richardson-Merrell had set for the release of Kevadon was long past, and in October 1961 Kelsey was still refusing to license the drug. The company executives were keen to have the drug on the market in time for Christmas, a notable period of stress, but on 18 October news broke linking thalidomide to certain birth defects. On 29 October Chemie Grünenthal notified Richardson-Merrell that thalidomide had been withdrawn from the German market.

Frances Kelsey was hailed as a heroine when the extent of the thalidomide tragedy became common knowledge and was honoured by the government of the day, but the United States did not completely escape the thalidomide horror. Richardson-Merrell had conducted human trials that were not covered by FDA legislation in the period before applying for its licence for Kevadon. These trials included various patient groups, including pregnant women. The slipshod, careless practices of Chemie Grünenthal were repeated in that the trials were not conducted under rigorous medical supervision but were left in the hands of the company's sales and marketing department. A total of 2.5 million tablets were given out to thousands of patients via around 1,000 doctors. The tablets varied in colour and size and were unlabelled, so later identification proved extremely difficult. As in Germany, no systematic recording of prescription or results was done, and Richardson-Merrell was later unable to identify all the doctors who had been given the samples.

Frances Oldham Kelsey

As a result eleven mothers were officially recorded as having thalidomide babies, but it is likely that these represent only the tip of the iceberg. It's a known fact that many thalidomide babies did not survive to term, were stillborn or died shortly after birth – in which case their deaths would have been recorded before the knowledge of the effects of thalidomide broke. Just like my own mum and dad, many parents would be unaware that their damaged children were the result of the toxic action of thalidomide and wouldn't have come forward to identify themselves. However, it is clear that, but for the obstinate attention to regulation and the refusal to be intimidated or to compromise demonstrated by Dr Kelsey, there would have been a disaster of epic proportions for the American nation.

Approximately two tons of Kevadon remained unaccounted for in the US even after the threat of thalidomide was revealed. My mother still had a bottle containing a Distaval tablet in her kitchen cupboard more than three years after I was born. Thalidomide was an over-the-counter remedy in many countries and a prescription drug and a hospital sample in many others. How many tablets continued to be swallowed with devastating but unrecognised and unreported results in the years following the drug's withdrawal? How many more bottles or packets may still to this day be lurking in the world's medicine cabinets or at the back of hospital shelves? It doesn't bear thinking about, does it?

It wasn't until the summer of 1961 that voices linking thalidomide to birth defects began to be heard. Parents who bore a child with a birth defect, like my parents, simply assumed it was something genetic or a one-off tragedy. They were unlikely to meet other parents with similar children, but in fact that is what eventually happened and that is how the disaster first came to light.

Dr William McBride, an Australian obstetrician practising in Sydney, attended the births of three babies with similar malformations during May and June of 1961. Such malformations are normally extremely rare. All three died soon after birth and Dr McBride, puzzled and alarmed by these events, took the children's medical records home to see if there was any common factor that might account for the deformities. He found that all three mothers had taken Distaval during their pregnancies.

Dr William McBride:
Picture source: Keystone
Press Agency.

McBride had earlier read academic papers regarding the potential of drugs to affect the foetus and cause birth defects. Convinced that thalidomide had caused the malformations, he immediately persuaded the Crown Street Women's Hospital in Sydney to stop prescribing Distaval. He also wrote a paper about it, which he sent to *The Lancet* medical journal (and which, unfortunately, was not published). More time elapsed, with thalidomide still on sale, before the terrible truth was finally exposed. McBride also contacted Distillers' sales department and passed on his fears but it seems no one reacted, as nothing was done

Lawyer Karl Shulte-Hiller's sister gave birth to a baby with short flipper-like arms at about the same time in Germany. Shulte-Hiller then feared for his own wife, who was pregnant with their first child… with good reason as, unbelievably, she gave birth a few weeks later to a daughter with the same defects. Stunned, Shulte-Hiller went to see Professor Widukind Lenz, a paediatrician at Hamburg University to seek an explanation.

When he showed the doctor his daughter's X-ray the amazed medic was able to show him an almost identical X-ray of another child, which he had received only that morning. Clearly something very strange was going on. The two men then set out to discover if there had been any other similar cases in recent months.

Meanwhile, back in Australia – with no response to his alarm calls over thalidomide – William McBride conducted some tests on animals but was unable to create teratogenic effects because, unknown to him, the susceptibility of most species used for lab testing was much less than the human susceptibility to the drug. McBride began to doubt his own beliefs until two more deformed babies were born at the Crown Street Hospital in September. He then contacted Distillers again, once more voicing his fears.

Professor Widukind Lenz

At the same time Lenz had discovered eight cases of phocomelia in Hamburg over the previous two years, a fantastically high percentage compared to naturally occurring rates. As his suspicions grew he discovered a paper written by a Dr Wiedemann that detailed twenty-seven cases in the area of Kiel, and which suggested that a new drug might be responsible. Lenz began interviewing the mothers of these babies and soon discovered they had taken thalidomide during their pregnancies. In November he contacted Dr Mückter at Chemie Grünenthal and told him that Contergan should be withdrawn immediately. He followed this up with a written letter, but Chemie Grünenthal took no action.

In Australia Dr McBride met with a Distillers sales manager to discuss his fears about Distaval. He also wrote again to *The Lancet*, and this time the letter was published a month later. It is dreadful to think how the process of discovery lumbered on, taking ages to gain public attention. During all that time pregnant women were still taking thalidomide under one name or another, with catastrophic results.

In Germany Lenz attended a conference in November where a paper was presented on birth defects, and Lenz informed the assembled doctors that a recently introduced drug was responsible for the outbreak of phocomelia. The next day three Grünenthal representatives met with Lenz and the Hamburg authorities and were asked to withdraw Contergan in the light of Lenz's evidence. Instead they refused, threatened Lenz with legal action and sent out a flood of promotional letters to doctors that avowed the safety of their product. Further meetings were held in which Chemie Grünenthal was ordered by the authorities to take Contergan off the market, but Dr Mückter steadfastly refused to do so. It was only when a major German newspaper reported Lenz's findings on 25 November, which emphasised that further delay on the company's part meant more deformed births, that Chemie Grünenthal agreed to withdraw Contergan. Even then they only consented to remove it from the German market, while continuing to sell it abroad.

The company then instructed its scientists to begin animal tests to see if Contergan could cross the placenta, and thus have the potential to affect the foetus in the womb. The results showed that it could. Separate research conducted by Lenz established the window in pregnancy when this might occur. It was a surprisingly small period in which to produce such devastating effects. The drug needed to be taken between the twentieth and thirty-sixth day of pregnancy, a point so early on that women taking the drug may not have even been aware that they were pregnant. After this period the drug was safe in terms of its capacity to cause birth defects, though its capacity to cause peripheral neuritis would remain.

As Brynner and Stephens (2001) note it was the power of the popular and medical press that finally caused Chemie Grünenthal to capitulate, while official bodies had largely stood by or proved ineffectual. This situation would be repeated in Britain in the 1970s when compensation was sought. At the beginning of December 1961 DCBL decided to withdraw Distaval in the UK (pending further investigations as a result of the overseas reports). However, it seems that it was still supplied to hospitals, which requested it as late as 1962 (The *Sunday Times* Insight Team, ibid.).

Like Frances Kelsey in the US, William McBride was hailed as a hero. He was named Australia's man of the year in 1962 and was made a CBE by Queen Elizabeth II in 1969.

Brynner and Stephens (ibid.) put the total of thalidomide babies at 8,000–12,000, with 5,000 surviving to adulthood. In their book The *Sunday Times* Insight Team put the figure higher, at around 8,000 survivors worldwide. No one really knows how many died *in utero*, or how many were born dead or dying. And there must be many cases that have never been reported, so these figures may at best be regarded as conservative.

When DCBL withdrew Distaval they stated that it was only a precautionary measure in response to international uncertainty, and that the evidence against thalidomide was of a circumstantial nature. They stressed that there had been no reports of birth defects in the UK. Of course this was because the parents then did not know what had caused their offspring's terrible injuries.

Some did not find out for many years after their child was born, but once realisation hit home – and, more importantly, once they discovered they were not alone but in fact formed a sizeable group – the parents began to ask questions and organise themselves.

My parents were part of this growing movement, but of course I was then oblivious of the whole thing. I don't think anyone sat me down and explained it all to me until I was much, much older. I only recall that I was the way I was and I didn't think too much about it. In 1962 I was enjoying life to the best of my ability, growing up in a world full of love and preparing to meet the wider society. Soon I would be going to school.

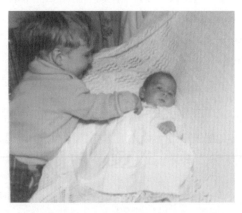

Me admiring Karen soon after she was born.

Chapter 4

David and Goliath

Scorpio people are characterised as strong, motivated non-quitters. They are fearless beings who are determined to succeed, and I think I can say I'm no exception to the rule. I certainly needed these qualities when I emerged from the shelter of my family and started school.

I went to Tiber Street Primary School off Lodge Lane. My mum had stuck out against the authorities for me to go to an ordinary school, and she was supported by Mr Dwyer from Alder Hey Children's Hospital. When I was tested at five, and found to have the IQ of an eight-and-a-half-year-old, any opposition caved in and I got the chance of an ordinary education. I think this has given me a major advantage in life over some thalidomiders who went to special day or residential schools. It enabled me to take part in the rough and tumble of normal life, to rely on my own abilities and stand my corner. These are qualities that have served me well in adult life.

I did get mollycoddled by the teachers though, much as I did at home. I was one of the best-behaved kids in the infants, and there was no sign yet of the hooligan I would later become. I was terrified of being naughty in case they told my dad, as I knew I would catch it when I got home.

Tiber Street was only over the road from our house so my mum was able to come in at break times and help me with using the toilet, or I might be allowed to run home instead. At lunchtime my food would be cut up for me by Ethel Webb, one of the school dinner ladies. Ethel lived in one of the police houses at the bottom of our street. She and her husband George always made a fuss of me, and I became mates with their sons Ian and Kevin. Ethel always looked out for me when I was small, picking me up when I fell off my bike and taking me into her house for much-needed first aid. When it was dinner time at school she would bring my plate over to me so I wouldn't have to struggle with it. There was no fuss or song and dance about it. She just did it matter-of-factly. It felt good having someone who knew me and my family to look out for me at school – someone from our street who understood me, not some stranger. They were great people, Ethel and George, but sadly now they are both long gone. It was through their son Ian that I met my wife Shelagh, but that is a story for later in this book.

My mum encouraged me to try to do things myself, but I always relied on her for help with washing and dressing. So, although I was independent in many ways, I perhaps never developed dexterity in the skills of daily living that were taught to disabled children in residential homes.

I hadn't had many chances to play with other children before I went to school except for those I met in hospital, and they mostly had problems of their own. I remember that when I was very small and I began to realise I was physically different from other kids I told myself I would be just like them, play like them and so on. I was determined that I would be the same as everybody else, but I got a rude awakening when I landed in a class full of ordinary kids. Obviously I got called names: 'Spaz', 'Flid' and suchlike. It was cruel, but I soon learnt I had to stand up to them. I could give as good as I got and better, verbally. I soon learnt to sharpen my tongue and use my wit. They used to call me 'Skippy' because of my short arms. Remember *Skippy the Bush Kangaroo*? I didn't let it get me down. After all, Skippy was a big hero, wasn't he?

Another tactic that has been my saviour is humour. Taking the piss out of myself before someone else can takes away their hurtful weapon and leaves them confused. I'd joke about my arms – say daft things, like I'd stuck my fingers in the jam – and it stopped people having a go at me. There wouldn't be any point. Little did I know that sense of humour would set me on a major career path later in life.

In any case I didn't have too many options. Tiber Street was a tough school in a tough district of a tough city. It was inevitable that I would be an attraction for bullies as the odd one out. I couldn't hope to win in a punch-up. With arms like mine the bully would practically have to put his chin in my face for me to reach him and I had no chance in a wrestling match, so I developed my best-ever defence mechanism: my big mouth. I grew adept at barbed wisecracks, and while they were reeling from my vicious verbal delivery I would run like hell. I was pretty fast on my feet.

However, I couldn't solve all my problems with words,

and there were many times when things got physical. I would come home with no arse in my pants and cut knees where I'd been ragged round the playground. I got into trouble for fighting, but I didn't care. I knew I had to stand up to the bullies. Luckily my mum understood. She'd say,

'You've got a good head and a good pair of legs. Go and give them what they gave you.' It may sound horrendous but I was learning to live and make my way in the ordinary world, and I'm so grateful to my mum for making sure I got that chance.

Because of my short arms and the repeated surgery I wasn't able to take full advantage of playtimes and sports session, but as I grew stronger and my arms developed I was more able to take part. Sometimes other kids didn't want me on their side or in their team when we played games, but if I felt rejected I never let it show. I had to make sure I wasn't the weakest in the bunch. In those early years I earned respect, but it was hard.

Luckily my teachers, Mr Bath and Mrs Cole, treated me the same as everyone else, except for the few concessions regarding toileting and mealtimes. However, they must have been aware of what was going on in the background, of my fight against the bullies and my efforts to stand up for myself. On one occasion my mother and I were out shopping for school clothes when we met Mr Bath, who recommended I got a clip-on tie and bought one for himself at the same time. On the Monday morning at assembly Mr Bath called Faley Woods (the worst of the playground bullies) up on the podium, and called me out too. He then announced a competition to take off an item of clothing, with second helpings of pudding at lunch for the winner. My heart sank. It was obvious I had no chance unless he chose shoes. Why was Mr Bath making a show of me like this? When he said 'necktie', though, I was laughing. I whipped mine off and came first, with Mr Bath a close second. Faley was left fumbling like a fool with his choking tie. Was his face red! To hammer the point home Mr Bath's lesson that morning was about David and Goliath.

I always like to win but I know how it feels to be the butt of other people's jokes, so I let Faley save face by giving him one of my prize puddings at lunch. Diplomacy was another skill that I was learning fast. I am a bad loser, but once victorious I can afford to be gracious.

Like my mum, Mr Bath always encouraged me to try to do things, to take a challenge. If it was something I didn't want to do I'd sometimes fall back on my disability as an excuse, but he wouldn't let me get away with that. Of course I did miss quite a lot of school because of being in hospital so often. We had classes in Alder Hey Children's Hospital, but they weren't really up to standard. Luckily I am quick to pick things up and found it easy to catch up, so I didn't fall behind the other kids. I didn't like school, though. It was always a chore. My mum and dad used to give me the guff that parents do about schooldays being the happiest of your life, and I used to say,

'Well, you go, then. I'd rather stay home.' Still, I kept up with my work and behaved myself, at least in primary school.

At home I was old enough to play outside by now, and I was football mad. At times my mum would worry about me being out in the street but my granddad, Pa Skyner, would say,

'Let the lad play out,' whereas if my dad came home and found me playing out he would immediately send me inside. I felt as if he didn't want me out in the street where people could see me – see the imperfect son he'd produced. Pa Skyner was great. He took me out to the park and other places and he'd give me a kickaround with a ball. When I got older and got a bike I'd always go to him if it needed fixing. He'd suck his teeth, pull a sorry face and make a song and dance about what a job it would be… but half an hour later he'd call me and the bike would be mended.

He partly made up for the love and companionship I

always felt I'd missed out on from my dad who, as soon as he came in, seemed to put a damper on things. I'd ask my dad to take me to the park but, if he did, he didn't really talk to me or play with me like other kids' dads. I remember him taking me one time and spending the whole time washing his car. Every Bonfire Night I'd ask for fireworks for my birthday but he always refused, saying it was a waste of money and he'd rather set fire to a twenty pound note.

When I was small Dad was someone to be worshipped, but I was in awe of him. Dads were like TV heroes – brave, but lovable – yet my dad always seemed distant. I never felt a bond of love between us. There were no all-boys-together times. He wouldn't take me to footy matches. Again, he saw these as a waste of time. Whenever he saw me it seemed to be time for bed. When we went on holiday he would tell me to walk ahead and not get under his feet.

But, to me, there seemed to be a more sinister side to him. On one occasion, when my mum was out and I needed help to get off the toilet, I called him but he didn't come. I was left sitting there for ages till my mum got back and found me shivering with cold. Dad was still in his armchair downstairs, oblivious to my cries for help.

I was frightened of the dark when I was little, and I would plead for a light to be left on in my room and the door to be left open. Sometimes I would shout down to Mum, just to reassure myself that she was there, but Dad would rush up and threaten to put a bolt on the door if I didn't shut up. It was his way of getting compliance: to threaten, rather than to soothe or cajole. Sometimes he would thump me through the bedclothes, although he would never hit me directly. Other times he would force me to drink a tot of whisky to make me go to sleep. But worst of all were Saturdays, when I would be left with Dad while Mum went shopping. Sometimes Dad would play-wrestle with me on the carpet, but he began putting a cushion over my face and holding it there a little longer each time he did it. Was it just accidental play, or not? I could never be sure, but I began to be afraid of being alone with him.

So my relationship with my father was precarious and often frightening. The father figure I looked up to in my formative years was my Grandpa Skyner, who became so important to me. As I got older and saw the love and fun other boys had with their fathers this divide worsened.

Another father figure entered my life when I became friends with John Smith. His father, also John Smith, always treated me the same as his own son. When I grew up we became good friends and he has remained with me, to this day, my best mate.

Me with John Smith Snr. (centre) and Charlie Wright (the Malteser Kid).

Charlie Wright is another great bloke I remember from those childhood days. In fact if fate had played a different hand he could have been my dad, as at one time he went out with my mum before she met my dad. In fact he went out with every one of the Ellis sisters. They used to compare notes on him after their dates. He played the same trick every time. He would take them to the pictures and buy them a big box of Maltesers, but he always ended up eating them all himself. They used to call him the Malteser Kid.

My first best mate was Billy Berry, who lived two doors away from us, but he got a brain disease when he was very young – only about six or seven. It made me hurt really bad to see him like that. He couldn't even speak, and he used to have a bed downstairs. He did eventually get his voice back, and I used to go to see him and take him little presents and sweets. We were like bosom buddies, and if he'd lived I think we would have stuck together and I wouldn't have needed other friends. He was my best mate, my playing mate… but I lost him.

I had lots of other friends as a child. I've always made friends easily, maybe because of my sense of humour. I didn't bother much with girls, and Karen and I never got on well enough to play together much. We both had volatile tempers – still have – so we were always fighting.

Me with Karen

When I got a bit older I had crushes on certain girls and I'd write them letters, but they wouldn't reply. They just sort of blanked me. I never really had a girlfriend all the time I was at school. If I phoned a girl up and she chatted to me I'd kid myself that we were going out together, but it just didn't happen. I think that because of my arms my disability was a barrier they didn't know how to cross.

Things improved a bit when I got to about fifteen – but when I was younger I wasn't too bothered, anyway. I pretty well lived for football, and used to spend a lot of my summer holidays at the Liverpool football ground. The problem with football was that no one ever wanted to pick me to be in their team in case my disability let the side down. It was only in desperation, when there was no one else to choose, that I was occasionally given a game. Then I went all out to prove I could play as well as anyone else, but it took a long time before I was accepted as a serious player.

*Mum, my Gran Skyner and Granddad Skyner
with Karen and me enjoying the sea air at Bangor,
North Wales in 1965.*

By the age of eleven I was making my way in the outside world at school and getting along pretty well. Surgery and physio had enabled me to manage my disability much better, as I became stronger and my muscles developed. Although there were tensions within the family I felt we had a pretty settled way of life, but it just goes to show how mistaken you can be. One day, without any warning, my dad left home. This was an event that would change our lives forever.

When I look back now I believe I must have seen it coming, but back then it was a terrible shock. Even though I was never really happy in Dad's company – and was even at times afraid of him – he *was* my dad, and in those days everybody had a dad and a mum who lived together.

I'll never forget the night he didn't come home. Karen and I had our bath and Mum got us in our pyjamas, and when it came time for her to read us a story he still wasn't home so I said,

'Where's me dad?'

and Mum said, 'He's not coming home.'

I said, 'Why, is he working away?'

Mum said, 'No, he's not coming back.'

Right away I guessed what had happened. I said,

'He's gone off with Marge, hasn't he?'

'How do you know that?' Mum asked. She was shocked but it all fell into place for me, even though I was so young.

Marge and her husband Tom were friends of Mum and Dad, and they used to go to the pub together. I'd noticed how he'd wink at her when he'd light her cigarette, so I sort of knew something was going on. My mum hadn't noticed anything, and she was so surprised that I had.

'Why didn't you tell me?' she asked, but I hadn't wanted to say anything. I didn't want to cause trouble, and perhaps I thought that if I didn't say anything nothing would happen.

However, trouble there was. Apparently Tom had rung my mum that morning and told her that Marge was leaving him. My mum, thinking he'd rung her for advice, tried to console him but he broke in on her well-meaning sympathies to tell her that Marge was running off with my dad. My mum couldn't believe her ears. Her whole world shattered in that instant. She flew up the stairs where my dad was standing on the landing looking sheepish, unable to deny the truth. She hit him as hard as she could, and that was the end of it. Twelve years of marriage and all the struggles they'd had together to bring me up were gone in a moment of anger.

When he left she planned to keep the truth from us, and to tell us he'd got a job working away and would only be able to see us at weekends. It would never have worked, but she was trying to protect us. Obviously it wouldn't wash now she realised I already knew, but she could still hardly believe that I had picked up on it while she hadn't suspected that anything was amiss.

Maybe she was too involved in looking after me to notice, and maybe that is one of the reasons it happened in the first place. I've thought about why it happened long and hard for many years. I even tried to talk to my dad about it, but I still don't really understand how he could have left us like that.

I cried my eyes out that night. Of course my first thought was that it was my fault, and even now I still can't shake the feeling that if I had been normal my parents would still be together today. My mum always said that it was nothing to do with me and it was just because of Marge, but I can see it wasn't as simple as that. I'd always known that he couldn't come to terms with me, that I was a burden to him and he was ashamed of my imperfection. I try not to blame him for this. One thing people don't realise is the amount of stress that falls on the rest of the family with a disabled member: there are mental as well as physical stresses. It took me a long time to realise that many other thalidomide families went through similar (and often worse) destruction. In some cases the children were put into care and rarely visited by their parents. In many others the family split apart. Like in mine, it was usually the fathers who left. Even when you know it's something that happened to a lot of other people it doesn't stop the unique hurt you feel for yourself and your own family.

The psychological issues surrounding the thalidomide tragedy are very complex, with immense implications. There were huge guilt trips for the parents who brought the children into the world and for the medical professionals who advocated and prescribed the drug – and also for the children themselves, who were continually conscious of the strains they put on those they dearly loved and on the rest of society.

On top of that there's the social rejection shown towards imperfect beings. The horror shown towards thalidomide children is particularly strong. Some parents couldn't bear to look at their children. Some even committed suicide to escape. Even hardened health professionals seemed to demonstrate a horror of the thalidomide victims, and tended to encourage parents to put their children away into institutions. We were at times referred to as 'monster babies' (the term 'teratogenic' is derived from the Greek for 'monster'). So, as I grew, I came to know that other people went through the same things and that what my dad did was a common occurrence.

I feel sorry for him and for all the others who suffered similar anguish and I try to understand their reactions, but what happened to me hurts and hurt makes me angry. I'm angry on behalf of all those who have had to live through this disaster, and I'm angry at the people and the organisations that caused it. It also makes me determined to succeed in whatever I set myself to do, to prove wrong all those people down the line who have said, *He (or she) will never amount to much.* All those people are in my mind, spearheaded by my own father, a ghost figure I fear I will never be able to lay to rest.

My mum was always by my side, from right after I was born until the day she died, and she really didn't have time for anybody else. It was as if she thought, *I made him, gave birth to him. It's my job to do the best I can for him.* I guess my dad and Karen got left out and felt neglected.

Years later my dad told me that Mum would never go out with him for a night out and that they had no social life together, so I suppose I can see how he was easy meat for another woman. He once told me that I was the 'other man' in their marriage. I can understand that now, but it doesn't mean I can forgive him for the way he left us in the lurch.

I've wondered about whether Dad blamed Mum for taking thalidomide, but I think first and foremost that he always had that lingering thought that he was somehow responsible himself – that his belief in his own manhood was compromised, and I was a constant reminder of it. Maybe he also thought the same about Mum, that she'd borne him a deformed son. I don't really know. I know that our GP, Dr Bruce, when other health officials were running around hiding the evidence and passing the buck, sat my dad down and explained it all fully to him. He explained how it was no fault of his or Mum's, or even of the doctor's himself, who had acted in good faith when prescribing the tablets on the advice of the pharmaceutical companies. After that I think he felt better but I still think he couldn't lose that feeling of inadequacy around me, and I'm sure he blamed her for making me the centre of her life.

Apparently the affair had been going on for years, since around the time Karen was born, and once my mum found out all about it she was understandably very bitter towards both Dad and Marge. She'd thought of Marge as a friend, and to discover this had gone on behind her back all this time shattered her emotionally. It was as if they'd made a fool of her, because she hadn't noticed what was going on… although once she found out she kept remembering little things and kicking herself for not putting two and two together. I think also that she did really love him and I feel she still carried a torch for him years later, despite all the bitter things she said at times.

Over the years I've realised what complex issues were involved, but at the time I just wanted him to come back. It was an odd thing, really. I was always in awe of him but I kind of hero-worshipped him at the same time. Maybe it was that I had this idealised image of what a dad should be and I kept hoping he would turn out to be like that. Some hope.

After he left us he went to live in a flat on the Wirral. Maybe he thought it would be far enough away for us not to be able to get at him. I still kept hoping he would come back, and then he did for a short while. I thought everything was going to be OK but then Marge kept phoning him and threatening to put her head in the gas oven, and so he went back to her.

I was heartbroken. I missed that father figure, but gradually I realised that his absence gave me new freedoms. There was no more lying in bed, listening to other kids playing out at night, or having to stay home while my pals were playing in the park. I'd ask if I could go, expecting to be refused, and Mum would say,

'Go on, son,' and I'd say,

'Eh?' I'd be really taken aback. She'd let me try things that Dad always said I wouldn't be able to do, like climbing trees. She'd just tell me to be careful. Sometimes Dad would be right and things would be beyond me, but at least now I got the chance to find out for myself. I was free to try as much as I could and accept the things I couldn't do, and make the most of the things I could. I realised I was on to a winner. Life was improving for me, and I started to think, *I hope he never comes back*.

We used to see him for visits on and off, but Marge did her best to discourage him. I always thought she was a horrible woman, and she was always stand-offish with us. Gradually the visits tapered off, and in the end they emigrated to Australia. I think she was unsure of her hold over him and saw us as a threat, and I think the decision to go to Australia was to get him as far away from us as she possibly could. Eventually we more or less lost touch and, even now, I have as little contact as possible. I could never understand what he saw in her.

Despite my new freedom it was hard for us after he left. He didn't make financial provision for us, and Mum had to go to work in the hospital to support us as well as trying to bring us up on her own. If it hadn't been for my grandpa and Grandma Skyner I don't know how we would have managed. They were a great help to her and my Grandpa Skyner became the father figure I'd always wanted, and was much loved by me for the loving care he gave me.

Albert (Pa) Skyner

My mum was so strong for us, and she was always there for me no matter what. I was always, and remain, so proud of her. At that point we still hadn't had a penny in compensation, even though the thalidomide parents had begun their collective fight in 1962. I still knew very little about it. No one had ever explained to me why I had to have all these operations, and the only help we got was that a minibus from the Lady Hoare Thalidomide Appeal would pick me up and take me to my hospital appointments. I'd see the word 'thalidomide' written on the side of the van, but I didn't know what it meant and never thought anything about it. However, unknown to me, Mum and Dad had already spent years in a wearying battle against Distillers for compensation.

My dad, with his clerical background, had shouldered the responsibility for doing the running round to meetings and negotiations and maybe that just put one more nail in the coffin of their marriage. Maybe he just got fed up with nothing happening after years of effort and no sign of any money (which would have made all our lives easier). I think he just couldn't be arsed any more, and was enticed away to greener pastures.

In Germany, almost as soon as thalidomide was withdrawn, the public prosecutor's office in Aachen began investigations with a view to proceeding with a criminal prosecution against Chemie Grünenthal's executives. It took four years to build their case, but no other authority in the world took such action on behalf of the victims.

Gathering information was slow. This was partly due to Chemie Grünenthal's refusal to give up documents and records for examination but also due to the fact that in many cases there were no records. Thalidomide samples had been handed out indiscriminately, so there was difficulty in identifying thalidomide children.

The trial was not ready to begin until 1968, by which time I and most of the other thalidomide children were around nine years old. It was a massive operation, and was almost as huge as the Nuremberg trials. Nine Chemie Grünenthal employees were indicted, but two were excused on health grounds. The others included Heinrich Mückter and Hermann Wirtz, who were charged as follows:

1. That they put on sale a drug which, even when taken according to instructions, caused an unacceptable degree of bodily harm.
2. They failed to test it properly.
3. They advertised it as safe when they could not guarantee that it was.
4. It caused people who took it to itch, shake, sweat, vomit and suffer peripheral neuritis.
5. They suppressed reports of adverse reactions and lied to doctors who asked questions.
6. The drug caused many cases of malformed babies.

Chemie Grünenthal's defence was that there was no proof that thalidomide had caused the birth defects and, in any case, an unborn child had no legal rights and therefore it was not a criminal offence to administer a drug that caused defects. It just goes to show how callous and self-seeking the defendants were.

The trial dragged on for over a year, costing God knows how much until, in 1970, Grünenthal made an offer of compensation to the German thalidomide families on condition that they dropped any civil lawsuits. It then argued that if the criminal trial continued that it could last for many more years (with appeals procedures), and that the company would then be in danger of bankruptcy. In this event the families would get no compensation at all – that is, if they waited for the outcome in order to pursue civil suits. Accordingly, in 1970, the parents accepted Grünenthal's offer, which then put pressure on the authorities. Consequently, in December 1970 the court and prosecution agreed to suspend the trial indefinitely.

Although it was almost certain that the defendants would have been found guilty they had not legally been found responsible for the disaster, and never admitted liability. Thus no legal basis for compensation was set, and Chemie Grünenthal got off scot-free.

Similar problems were occurring in other countries, with civil cases dragging on for years while the thalidomide children were growing up without any financial help. When settlements did finally begin to be paid in the late 1960s they were generally too inadequate to compensate for the past and future needs of the children. I suppose, to be fair, the thalidomide disaster was something no one had had to deal with before. No one knew how long the children were likely to survive. However, I can't help feeling that the general hope of the distributors was that the longer the suits went on the fewer of us there would be left, so in a way dragging their feet was an exercise in damage limitation. The fact that many thalidomide children died at birth or in their early years meant that their families were never compensated at all.

Things were rather different in the USA, where personal injury litigation was a much more well-known and used procedure. Additionally, their lawyers were much more contentious than, for instance, those in the UK. Another factor was perhaps the very small number of thalidomide cases in the USA, thanks to the FDA's refusal to license the drug. Even so the distributor, Richardson-Merrell, followed the same route as the other conglomerates in trying to get away with the minimum payment possible.

For example Shirley McCarrick's daughter Peggy, who was born with a shortened leg and flipper-like foot was originally offered a measly $6,000. This was eventually increased by the court to $2.75 million, but this was later reduced to around $500,000. Still, it was a hugely larger figure than the first offer. As was typical of all the compensation claims the child was nine years old before any money was paid, and the mother had to overcome huge legal obstacles in order to pursue her claim properly.

On the other hand, it soon became obvious that the matter of compensation could not be settled quickly. It took several years for many of the parents to identify their children as damaged by thalidomide. The first few years after a thalidomide baby was born passed in a whirlwind of grief, shock and learning to love and care for their child. It was only once they gained knowledge of the chemical cause of their children's disabilities that they began to reach out to other families, to get angry and to seek redress.

Even once they realised they might qualify it was difficult to prove whether the injuries were caused by thalidomide or by some natural flaw. The drug had been released under different names and in different shapes and colours in different countries. It was also available in syrups and mixtures as well as tablets, so a lot of people didn't realise what it was they had taken. How many people read medicine information leaflets thoroughly?

On top of that, in many countries thalidomide was available as an over-the-counter remedy for a range of minor conditions. So people probably forgot that they had taken it at all, or didn't count it as a medication when asked.

This sorry state of affairs indicated that it would take a long time to sort out what compensation should be paid. No one knew how to calculate the future costs of care for the families so time would be necessary to work out how the children would develop, what their needs were likely to be and their estimated life expectancy. The usual way of dealing with this is for interim payments to be made to ease the victims' difficulties while negotiations proceed, but this didn't seem to happen anywhere and, for the most part, no one received a penny until the children were verging on their teens.

In 1961, when I was two years old, one parent wrote to Enoch Powell, the then health minister, demanding to know what he intended to do about Distillers Company (Biochemicals) Ltd and the thalidomide scandal. This letter remained unanswered, so the mother contacted her local newspaper. The paper then carried her story, which provoked an immediate response from the Ministry of Health. Their reply, which obviously took the view that the tragedy was an act of God rather than the result of negligent practice, was that DCBL could not be held responsible for the unforeseeable side effects of thalidomide. Articles then began to appear in the national press endorsing the government view, but a group of MPs disagreed and asked Powell to invoke a public enquiry.

Powell refused to do this, but at this point the parents were beginning to realise through the press reports that they had a common cause and a group formed. They appealed to the minister but Powell adopted an unsympathetic, if not hostile, attitude. He refused to meet any of the children, and intimated that people who took medication of any kind had only themselves to blame for any adverse reactions. At a meeting with the parents he refused to take any action. One parent recalled him saying,

'I hope you're not going to sue for damages; no one can sue the government' (The *Sunday Times* Insight Team, 1979, p. 143).

This decision meant that no official examination into DCBL's conduct would be made and, therefore, what had happened would not be brought to public notice. The families would have to seek redress through the civil courts, whose process effectively curtailed any power of the press to make the affair public. The laws of contempt would prevent release of any information while lawsuits were ongoing. The strength of public opinion would thus be denied to the parents, who would have to soldier on, relying on their legal representation to fight their corner.

Despite the fact that everything seemed heavily weighted against them this small group of parents took the decision to sue DCBL in August 1962. Four families came together and, as news spread, others joined them and the Society for the Aid of Thalidomide Children was formed. Lady Hoare, wife of the Lord Mayor of London, became its president and chairman and she also set up the Lady Hoare Thalidomide Appeal to gather funds for the children. It was this society that my parents were told about when they learnt that I was a thalidomide child, and they then joined the group.

The problem with the Society was that its premise was based on charitable action rather than the legal rights of the families and compensation. Its focus was really on assisting the families to deal with the practical and emotional problems they faced. Any funds went into providing practical help, like the minibus that used to take me to hospital appointments, and the matter of legal redress was left for the parents to sort out by themselves.

There was also an association called the Kevin Club which was more local to me, having been founded by a doctor at Alder Hey Children's Hospital. He collected information about all the children born in the area with thalidomide defects, but this organisation was also biased towards charitable assistance and discouraged parents from taking legal action.

However, it was probably only through these two societies that I began to become aware of what had happened to me. Through their activities I began to be introduced to other children like me. I remember they took a load of us on a bus to the circus at Belle Vue in Manchester (not to be in it, I hasten to add). It was a fifty-two-seater coach and it was chocka with fifteen to twenty thalidomide kids, their families and their carers, who were all from the north-west. I was about eight or nine and it was only then, when I saw them getting carried off the coach because they had no legs or arms, that I realised there were others a lot worse off than me.

There was also a holiday home in Jersey that was purpose-built, and a lot of the thalidomide kids used to go there. I never went, so I can't really say what it was like. I sort of distanced myself from other thalidomide kids. I didn't really consider myself as one. Never have done. Lots of thalidomide kids lived in care, and many hardly saw their parents. They must have felt they were ditched by them and so I think they developed a kind of a group family identity of togetherness. I think a lot of them still feel that way, as if they are a separate group in society with a common cause, if you like. I never had that because I lived in a normal family and social environment. I didn't identify myself that way.

*A school group of thalidomide children
around the mid 1950s*

Anyway, once the Thalidomide Society was formed, the parents involved began to think about how to get some recompense for their sufferings. Can you imagine the problems they faced in the early 1960s once the full horror of what had been done to them dawned?

The small number who came out of their isolation to form the Society in 1962 started the ball rolling but the parents had little experience of lawsuits, let alone taking on a huge conglomerate like Distillers. Don't forget that in those days the judicial system was more heavily weighted against working-class plaintiffs than it is today. Only the wealthy could afford to pay the huge legal costs involved in a suit, and you had to apply for a legal aid certificate – which, depending on the merits of your case – might or might not be granted. If it *was* granted you could be expected to pay towards the costs, even if your income was modest. There were none of the 'no win, no fee' arrangements that are popular today. Solicitors were not allowed to advertise their skills or tout for clients, and personal injury litigation was not the free-for-all that it is rapidly becoming.

The result was that, to most people, the legal system and its representatives were inaccessible and shrouded in mystery. Ordinary people had little idea of which lawyers might specialise in personal injury, or who best might represent their case.

It says a lot for the grit of that early group of parents who, while still wading through the uncharted territory of their children's needs, managed to stick together and confront the mighty Distillers company.

Chapter 5

Goals and Goalposts

I was thirteen before our family received a penny in compensation. Even though the first lawsuit was filed on 7 November 1962, the fact that the press was gagged by the contempt of court laws meant that it was a long time before all the families were able to find out what was going on and what they should be doing. The difficulties the first lawsuit encountered on all sides meant that the families concerned felt obliged to accept a very inadequate settlement in 1968 after it had dragged on for years.

However, the first lawsuit paved the way for a further wave of action, which finally began to open up the can of worms and reveal the ramifications of the thalidomide disaster. The first set of claimants consisted of only sixty-four families, but once they had reached a settlement many more cases materialised in the wake of the ensuing publicity. Unfortunately these new claimants (my parents among them) found that the time limit for bringing a civil action had by then expired, and they were told they had no legal right to sue. Luckily some parents refused to accept this. Spearheaded by David Mason, a London art dealer, whose daughter Louise was born without arms or legs, a successful campaign was mounted to obtain leave to sue for the remaining families.

After another long-drawn-out battle a settlement was drawn up for these families. Although the Hinchcliffe award for the first families worked out at just 40% of a total estimate of the children's lifetime needs (in some cases panning out at less than £10,000), these were lump sum settlements. In the 1972 proposals a sum of £3.25 million was to be shared among over 300 children, but this was to be invested in a trust fund to be doled out to the children as needed.

Again – if you think about it – it didn't add up to much, when you allowed for the expenses some families would incur. And it surely didn't recompense them for what they had already suffered.

The figures were more or less worked out between the groups of opposing lawyers during 1971, and again DCBL insisted on the payment being conditional on all parties accepting the offer. The majority of the families were by now fed up with the legal wrangling. Their lives had been on hold for years while endless negotiations and meetings went on, and some of them were desperate for financial help.

At this time most of us thalidomide children were in or approaching our early teens, and our parents were thinking of how to provide for our needs as adults – how to enable us to become independent. It was as if DCBL deliberately picked this time to make their offer – when the parents would be at their most vulnerable, and worrying how their children would cope as adults.

If you think that is a far-fetched suggestion then let me tell you about the letter that the parents received, dated 14 December 1972. Note that it was just before Christmas, a period of financial stress for most families. The letter set out the draft proposals for the trust to be set up the following year, and asked the parents to read them and take legal advice before signing. Also enclosed was a cheque for £500. The letter went on to say that they looked forward to receiving the signed documents, and wished the parents a happy Christmas. It then finished by saying that if the parents didn't sign the papers they should return the cheque. If that wasn't unfair pressure I don't know what is.

Most of them wanted to settle, but six families refused to do so. They were again spearheaded by David Mason, who was financially comfortable enough to be able to fight on.

All sorts of tactics were used by both sides to get the parents to sign. They were told by Kimber Bull, their own lawyers, that if they didn't sign they would lose their legal aid certificate. Tremendous pressure was put on these six families, with the implication that their behaviour was damaging all the other families – who, albeit reluctantly, were prepared to settle. My own parents were among this majority. At first my dad handled all this side of things but I think he got really fed up with it, and by now he was looking towards his new life with Marge.

Another worrying development was the announcement of an X and Y list being drawn up. Those on the X list were those who were accepted as, or who could prove they were, thalidomide damaged. Those with uncertain claims as to the cause of their deformities went on the Y list, which would obviously affect the amount of damages to be awarded. Most of the parents had not been told which list they had been allocated to before being asked to sign the agreement. Of course all these tactics served to divide the families and set them against each other, rather than against their common foe.

But the six families stood firm, which showed remarkable bravery. However, their own lawyers, who were supposedly acting on their behalf, responded with an unbelievable act of savagery. In a bid to solve the issue they took the six sets of parents to court to have their status as 'next friend' (meaning 'legally responsible for acting on behalf of their child') removed. When the case was heard it came before the same judge (Judge Hinchcliffe), who had earlier overseen the 1968 agreement to settle. He promptly allowed the action. This took away the parents' legal responsibility, which would then pass to government officials or to the Official Solicitor. No doubt the lawyers thought there would be no problem getting these officials to sign the agreement on behalf of the children.

Legal people tend to close ranks, and when some of the parents tried to instruct their lawyers to appeal they found them unwilling to continue representing them. Bewildered, heartsick and threatened with the possibility of legal costs which they couldn't pay, two of these courageous parents gave in and signed.

Fortunately David Mason had enough money and nous not to be fazed by it all, and he pursued and won an appeal against this disgusting ruling on behalf of the six families. However, DCBL still refused to pay out unless everybody signed, so there then followed a period of stalemate. Publicity might have forced the issue but the press was gagged while the matter was *sub judice*, and so the sordid game continued to be played out in secret.

At this point The *Sunday Times* came into the picture, and I think that without their help we would never have got a settlement. Since 1968 Harold Evans, the paper's editor, had been investigating and trying to publish details of the thalidomide story but had been mostly prevented from doing so by threats of action for contempt of court. Evans's investigation revealed the disgraceful treatment meted out to the families, and he wanted to take up a newspaper campaign on their behalf. But how could they evade the hobbling contempt laws?

Eventually Evans decided to take the risk, and on 24 September 1972 the paper published an article detailing how the justice system had failed the families. On 1 October it published a further article, which included letters and statements from some of the parents. These articles stimulated reaction in the wider press and among parliamentary members. It soon became obvious that the whole scandal was going to come out into the open.

Labour MP Jack Ashley ran an all-party campaign asking for moral justice for the families, which he hoped would force DCBL to make adequate settlement, but despite the building furore the company kept silent. Pressure was put on the Conservative government to take responsibility for the children, but this suggestion was rejected by Sir Keith Joseph. His argument was that it was a private matter between DCBL and the families, but he conceded that a government trust fund for the children would be considered once the litigation between the two parties was completed.

DCBL's public image was beginning to look pretty tarnished, especially in the light of their continued silence. While all this was going on posters began to appear all over the country publicising the thalidomide disaster and calling for boycotts of DCBL's products. They featured images of DCBL's most popular lines. No one knew who was producing the posters, but posterity attributes them to Robert Maxwell, the editor of the *News of the World*.

Although such a smear campaign might smack of cheap tactics, which were set apart from the serious matter of obtaining justice, it was probably highly effective in getting public attention. It must be said that only when the threat of a boycott became a tangible issue did DCBL, forced even by their own shareholders to do the right thing, finally bow to pressure. A DCBL Shareholders Committee was formed in November 1972 to exert pressure on the company. The shareholders may have been motivated by a desire for moral justice for the families, but also it was in their own interests to protect their investments. External pressure was building, with some supermarket chains now refusing to stock DCBL's products until they made a decent settlement. The company's share prices began to fall.

Front Cover of Private Eye, Friday 17 November 1972
Reproduced by kind permission of Private Eye magazine.

As a result – surprise, surprise – DCBL had a sudden change of heart. They withdrew the offer of £5 million and replaced it with a package worth £20 million, to be paid out over the next ten years. The final settlement reached in 1973 was for £6 million, to be shared between the outstanding 340 thalidomide children. This would give them payment equal to that received by the original 1968 claimants. And £2 million a year was to be paid into a trust fund for seven years to provide money for all the children's future needs. A further amount was put aside to pay for the operation of the trust. A clause was inserted into the agreement to allow up to 10% extra to be invested in the trust in the event of rising inflation.

Of course it still wasn't enough, and the families were disgusted to learn that any money the children received would be liable for income tax. The government added £5 million to the trust fund to offset this tax liability. In hindsight the amounts still were clearly inadequate for the level of lifetime care that would be required. Perhaps no one expected us to survive as long as we have, and probably no one imagined the degree to which inflation would eat away at the value of the fund. Still, at approximately £54,000 per child, the settlement was a lot more than the £7,500 that DCBL had tried to force the families to accept a year earlier.

When the settlement was made I was thirteen years old. It made little difference to me. My dad was still handling negotiations on my behalf and he put the money in trust for me until I was twenty-one. The parents themselves were given a lump sum of £5,000, and even though my dad no longer lived with us he fought tooth and nail to make sure he got half of it. I did get a yearly allowance but I had been assessed as less damaged than other children and I received a very low allocation, so our financial situation didn't change much. I used to get a clothes allowance, which was about £350 a year – quite a lot, in those days – and I used to go to town and blow it on expensive trainers and designer kitbags and stuff like that. I wasn't really aware of anything that had gone on – neither the battle for the money nor the struggles of the families. I was just a thirteen-year-old lad, and I had other things on my mind… mostly football.

After my dad left home my life revolved round my mum and my granddad, 'Pa' Skyner, who became, really, the father I'd never had. Mum, Karen and I were then living in Rundle Road, just round the corner from Aspen Grove. There was a scare in 1976 when my mum had Bell's palsy and she was very ill for a while, but as we went into the 1970s my life was for the most part pretty secure. I was the class clown at school, developing strategies to outwit any bullying with verbal weapons. I began to change from the conforming child I'd been at primary school, when I had been living in fear of my dad, to becoming a bit of a scallywag and trying to be the kid who was up for anything.

I'd not long been at secondary school. There was this old disused church near home. One time a few of us were playing up there and one of the lads threw a brick through the window. We all ran and Father Bunloaf, or whoever he was, came out and chased us. He knew which school we were from because we were all wearing our school blazers, but the only one he picked out was me. At the time we all got away, and I thought that was the end of it.

I was staying at my nan's in Aspen Grove and I'd forgotten all about it till the Saturday morning when I was still in bed and the police came knocking at the door. Apparently they'd been to my house first and when my mum opened the door they said,

'Mrs Skyner, we've come about young Gary.' My mum immediately thought something terrible had happened and fainted on the spot. Anyway, when she came to she told the police where I was and they came looking for me.

Now my nan was very clever – very astute – and she'd never take anything at face value. She wouldn't automatically take it as read that you were in the wrong, so she wanted to know first what I was supposed to have done. In those days hardly anyone had seen a thalidomide kid, so the description the police had was of a plump lad with short arms. In answer to my nan's questions they told her that I and my pals had been throwing bricks through the church windows. She then asked how high the windows were and how far they were from the street.

Once she'd got all that straight she knew I wasn't guilty, and she called me downstairs. I got halfway down, and once the coppers got a good look at me and my arms they just said,

'Forget it,' and left. My nan waited till they'd gone before she bollocked me. She said to me,

'Who did it?' and I said,

'Did what?'

She said, 'Don't go shielding people, and don't get involved with people who do things like that.' She was stern, my nan, but she would stick up for me if she thought I was in the right.

By this time I'd also become best mates with John Smith, a friendship that has withstood the test of time. I've already mentioned that John Smith's dad, who was also named John, was another substitute dad for me. I remember him giving John and me the registration fees so we could sign up for Sefton Park Rangers football team. John and I both wanted to sign up for the team but it cost fifty pence, and my mum was so hard up I didn't have the money. John said,

'Come on. We'll ask my dad,' and we went down to the Coach and Horses where John Smith Sr. was drinking with his mates. He gave me a big welcome and made a fuss of me, which surprised me as he showed no sign of being put off by my disability. He gave us a ten pound note and told us to get chips and curry and go home to watch the match on TV. I couldn't believe it. I don't think I'd ever even seen a ten pound note. Chips and curry only cost ten pence so we had lots left over, which we spent on illicit drinking and games of pool. Smithy, as I call him, has always had a reputation as a tough nut and a hard drinker but he is an instantly likeable person. He is very straight, and there is no one else I would rather call 'Dad.' He always treated us both the same, and he came to be a major figure in my life... and still is.

John Jr. was always over at our house, often with his brother Kevin. They all treated me as normal, which I really appreciated. John and I played for Sefton Park Rangers and then for Unity Boys club, and with this club we played on tour all over Europe. They were great times, and whatever I lacked in upper body strength I made up for in leg power. I remember, when I was twelve, playing for Sefton Park Rangers in a Cup Final when I scored a goal. I turned to the spectators to receive the expected roar of approval and at that moment John pulled my shorts down, revealing everything to the watching crowd. Of course I couldn't pull them up again, and was left begging my team mates to do it for me while they were all doubled up with laughter.

I was always hanging around Anfield. During the school holidays I'd jump the number 27 bus then catch the number 14 to the ground. I'd go to the matches too. In those days the entrance fee was affordable, not like now.

When I was fourteen I started my own football team out of Aspen Grove. I heard this bloke on Radio Merseyside – Joe May – saying they were looking for new teams to make up a league, so I phoned up. But it turned out he was from the Tuebrook area of Liverpool and only wanted teams from that district. However, he said that he would arrange some friendly matches for us and that maybe the following year their committee might consider taking teams from other areas.

After this I was contacted by a woman reporter from the *Catholic Pictorial*. She'd heard about me running the team and wanted to do a story about me. I was so proud when the article was published with a big photo of me in goal and saving a shot. I thought that was the end of it but she came and took me down to Anfield one Saturday morning. I thought she was just picking up tickets for her family or something. I couldn't believe it when Roy Adams met us at the door and then Bill Shankly came down the corridor and said,

'Come with me, son.'

Speechless, I followed him into this room and there were footy strips everywhere… hundreds of them. I had never seen so much red in my life. It was as if I'd died and gone to heaven. He gave me the full team strip, from number one right up to number fifteen, and he said to me,

'Look after these, son. Great people have graced this strip.' As you can imagine, I went home in a daze. It was a moment never to be forgotten.

When I was a little older I was in the 19th District Boys Brigade team, but I usually found myself in reserve. I used to sit on the bench counting how many players turned up. When it got to nine or ten my heart would start pounding, thinking I would get a go, but then another four would arrive and my hopes would be dashed. When I was very small and there were group games and things I'd never been left out like that. But as I grew older, and games became more competitive, people saw me as a handicap and often never gave me a chance.

One Saturday it snowed and only about six players turned up. It got to about twenty-five to three and I thought, *Coach is going to struggle to get a team together*. Then four more came in but they were still one short, and the one that was missing was the team's star player. By then it was ten to three and I thought *Fuck, I'm going to get a game*.

Mr Evans, the coach, came and said,

'Put your kit on,' and I thought, *Great*, but then he said,

'Wait in the dressing room because I'm expecting another player to come, but if he doesn't come by half-time I'll put you on.' He didn't want to put me on because he thought I'd let the side down and that it wouldn't look good, me having a handicap. His exact words were,

'It'll be a big psychological boost if the opposition see you instead of our star player.'

At half-time, however, he didn't really have any choice but to let me play. When I came on he'd never seen me play before. He'd just judged me on my arms. I hit the post after about seven minutes and then I scored a screamer, and he never left me out of the team again. Afterwards he said to me,

'I made a big mistake there. I just didn't think you were capable.'

I said, 'Well, I am,' and he said,

'I can see that now,' but I knew that if I hadn't got that

chance he would still have been doing that to me now. It's something I've had to fight all my life, that prejudging, from lots of people – not least from my own father. But I would do anything, especially where football was concerned, to prove I could do as well as anyone else.

This man, Peter Casey, came to my fiftieth birthday party. He'd been a teacher at my school and he told me what had gone on behind the scenes. They'd said,

'We're getting one of those thalidomide kids, and he's not to be treated any different from anyone else.' He said how they all used to watch me playing football in the schoolyard, and how I used to throw myself on the ground, on to hard concrete. He had everyone laughing at my birthday party, but it just goes to show how determined I was to succeed.

In 1975 I even got a trial for Liverpool. There were two other lads and me from our school: Mitchell Fletcher and Paul Scott. I was so excited I remember the date. It was 8 May. When we got to Anfield we were given a coaching session and then a competitive game.

Ronnie Moran was the coach that day, and at the end of the session he put his arms on my shoulders and he said to me,

'It's a pity about those arms. You realise you'll never make the grade, but if I had a first team squad with the same attitude as you we would win every game.' Of course I was disappointed, but his words went a long way to making me feel better. I told my mum what he'd said and she was as proud as I was.

Although I still loved to play I began to realise that I would be better placed in organising and coaching. I'd already run my own team and, at the age of sixteen, I lied about my age to take my preliminary FA coaching badge.

Chapter 6

The Grand National of Life

Arundel Comprehensive School Badge

Achieving has always been important to me in everything I do, and I felt so proud on the day I stood up to get my school leaving certificate at Arundel Comprehensive. When I was called up to the podium I stared out at the assembled pupils as Mrs Cope addressed them, saying,

'We are very proud of Gary and, let me tell you, there's nothing wrong with him. He is able-bodied when he wants to be and disabled when it suits him. Gary, you really have built the system here and played it to its maximum. I hope you continue to do so throughout your life.'

I knew she certainly had me down to a tee, but she had my best interests at heart. Her positive words were such a contrast to the sneers I had endured for years from my father. I stepped down, applause ringing in my ears, and made my way back to my seat. I sat misty-eyed, staring at the certificate that was evidence of the hard work I had put in to achieve an education. I thought back over all the obstacles that had been put in my way and all the things my father said I would never achieve and it came to me that life is like the Grand National. I might not win the race, but I would successfully complete the course. I had jumped this major hurdle but there would be many more to come, and experience had taught me to tackle adversities one by one.

I went home bursting with pride to receive more praise from my mum and my nan and Pa Skyner. I got more pleasure seeing the look on my mum's face than I did at my own achievement. It made me think about the time I got a bike for Christmas and my dad said I couldn't go out on it.

'You won't be able to ride it, anyhow,' he said, which was a typical instance of how negative he was about me. His words only made me more determined to succeed, so I crept out with the bike and tried to get the hang of it. Like all first-time riders I struggled, but because I couldn't reach the brakes with my arms I had to stop myself with my feet. My dad eventually came out and caught me and I got a right rollicking – on Christmas Day, too. I wondered what he would have to say if he could see me now I was leaving school on an equal footing with all the other kids in my class.

But leaving school and entering the world of work was a bit scary. Even though at that time there were still relatively plenty of job opportunities for young people I wasn't sure how well I would be accepted in a work environment.

Initially my career prospects were limited. Everybody insisted I would be best suited to some kind of clerical work, but that was hard for me to take. I'd come to terms with the fact that I would never be a career footballer but clung to my other lifelong aspiration – to be a fire bobby. I could have stayed on at school in the sixth form but a Miss Lester from the careers office in Old Hall Street contacted me with the suggestion that I might be trained as a telephonist, as I had a good telephone manner. She came to see me before I left school and we talked about different jobs I might do. I told her about my desire to join the fire service, and she said that if I trained as a telephonist I might be able to get a job in the fire brigade control room.

So when I left school in 1976 I started as a trainee on the switchboard at Alder Hey Children's Hospital, where I had spent so much time as a patient. I also gained some experience by training with the GPO at Exchange Flags in Liverpool and, after constantly writing to the fire service asking to be taken on, I finally got an interview in 1977.

I was interviewed by a very stern lady called Miss Fernio who, after putting me through a test, told me firmly,

'This is an emergency service, not a kindergarten. I'm very sorry, but you are far too slow. In my opinion, because of your disability, you wouldn't be able to get the fire engines out quickly enough.'

I was gutted but, never one to give up, I kept on applying. I have to say that my dad never ever gave me any help at all in finding a suitable job, even though he worked in the employment service and probably could have put in a word for me. I try to give him the benefit of the doubt by thinking that perhaps he wanted me to prove my independence.

Instead I got my MP, David Alton, to go with me on a

third interview at the fire service, but it didn't help. When we turned up Miss Fernio immediately said that she had already told me several times I was unsuitable. Mr Alton tried to help me out by saying my skills had speeded up since the previous interview, but she wasn't having it. It felt as if she had a downer on me and I felt so frustrated at the time, but later I had to admit that she had a point. The switchboards then were not computerised and involved a lot of reaching up and down pegging cables into holes, which I did find difficult. As I've said before, I hate to lose, but sometimes you have to face facts and change your goal.

My next job was also working a switchboard at Liverpool City Council's Municipal Buildings, an opening also found for me by Miss Lester. I passed the interview and the medical without problems, and started on my first fully paid job at a good wage of £39.90 a week. I was the only male operator working with seventeen women operators. It was heaven for a teenage boy, but I felt that I had only got the job because the supervisor felt obliged to take me on as part of the council's quota of disabled employees.

The family was delighted. My mum was over the moon, and at first everything was fine. But I soon began to have problems with the physical demands of the work. Some of the extensions were so high that I couldn't reach the holes to peg the cables in without standing up. While able-bodied operators could reach them sitting down, I was jumping up and down all day to get them in, which took a toll on my joints. My supervisor suggested I apply for a transfer to an easier job. I saw this as admitting failure and refused to give up. But after a few more months, and under pressure, I agreed to being transferred to a lighter job.

A funny thing happened to me while I was working there, though. Because of the way I have overcome disability at various times in my life I have often featured in media reports, and while I was working at the council switchboard the *Daily Mirror* published an article about my achievement in gaining employment despite being a thalidomide victim. Unfortunately they also included my name and full address and I was shortly introduced to the world of cranks, who like to pursue any kind of celebrity.

Within a few days of the publication this man phoned me and offered me a job paying three times what I was currently earning. He spoke with a cockney accent and told me the job involved delivering spools to film companies up and down the country. I was brooding on a change of job and had just passed my driving test, so this sounded quite exciting.

After several phone calls he rang me at work and asked me to meet him near Preston, but my supervisor was listening in on another line and she thought he sounded suspicious. She involved Merseyside Police and they told me they would tap my home phone, and when the man called they would listen in.

The next time he phoned I asked him why he wanted me to work for him when there were more experienced people available. After all, I was only a school leaver with little driving experience. At this he got suspicious and asked if the phone was being tapped. I said,

'Yes, the police are listening in.'

He said, 'Right, I'm going to get you now. You've had it.'

I hadn't been fully convinced that he was a crank until he started phoning my mum in the evenings before I got home from work and saying,

'I've got your boy. You'll never see him again.' My mum would be terrified, and would ring up work to see if I was still there.

It got really scary. Lancashire and Merseyside Police eventually got me to arrange a meeting with this bloke so they could arrest him. I had to go to Preston railway station to meet him but it all went wrong. The police arrested the wrong guy while the real bloke was watching from a distance. I knew this because the crank called me later and said,

'See, you're fucking scared. I was watching. The police are on to me. Well, you've had it now. I'm going to kill you.'

It upped the ante. It was one of the most frightening times of my life – remember, I was only a young lad. I kept getting these death threats from this complete nutter who I didn't know, had never met nor done any harm to. I didn't know what he looked like or anything, so every time I got on the bus to come home from work I was looking at every one I didn't know and thinking, *Could it be him?* One night I was coming home, walking down Aigburth Vale, and I asked this man the time and he answered me in a cockney accent. I shat myself, thinking this was the end, but it wasn't him.

In the end the police caught him. He was also making obscene phone calls to young women in Chorley. He was arrested and charged with making menacing phone calls to me and with threatening to kill me.

There have been other incidents over the years, which are inevitable when your name is in the public domain, but this one sticks with me because I was so young and naive at the time. What makes people behave in this way I don't know. I suppose we have to feel sorry for them, but they cause endless fear and distress to their victims and sometimes their fantasies spill over into real violence.

The year 1977 was an eventful year for me. I'd passed the exam to become a football referee and I also passed my driving test. I started taking lessons on my seventeenth birthday in 1976 and took the test just three months later in January 1977. It was great getting my first car (a brand-new Ford Escort) but I had to apply to the Trust for it, so it didn't actually belong to me.

First car for a young lad, 1977

That's one of the things that bugged me about the Trust Fund in those days: the fact that you had to go cap in hand for everything you wanted. I suppose it was to stop you wasting your money, especially when you were young, but it was a pain. I remember finding a letter in my records saying that they, along with my father, had tried to talk me out of getting a Ford Escort GL. They thought I should have the L model, but I'd been adamant about getting my own way. I think some of the other thalidomiders tend to rely on the Trust for advice in everything they want to buy or do, but I know my own mind. That's the way I've been brought up: to think for myself.

The year 1977 was also the year I got my first real girlfriend, but there was no sexual relationship and it didn't last very long. She was bound for a career in the police force, so for two reasons it was obvious we were going nowhere. The first reason was because all my mates would have gone mad if I'd started going round with a copper and bringing her into our drinking haunts and the second reason was because policewomen at that time were renowned for carrying on and having affairs and I didn't want that, so I ended it there and then. Really, I think it was mutual. I think she already had her eye on someone in the police force, but she wouldn't admit it.

It was around this time too that I started to become aware of what had gone on with DCBL and the compensation claims. I remember reading in the paper about a woman being awarded something like £200,000 because someone at her workplace called her a lesbian and I thought, *Fucking hell, we've had nothing like that.*

I was starting to understand how the families had been shafted after all they'd gone through – particularly my own mum, through no fault of her own. At this time, however, it seemed too big for me to get involved in and I had my own life to get on with. But the sense of injustice was building inside me.

Eventually I was moved from the council switchboard to a lighter job at Brougham Terrace, the site of the city's registry office. Instead of a fairly physical job and working in a group I sat all day near the door of the office, directing people to Births, Marriages and Deaths as required. I had to wear a uniform and it was pretty boring, really. I spent a lot of time reading the newspaper, but there were some funny moments too.

On one occasion I had to put out a fire after the cleaners had thrown an ashtray containing a smouldering cigarette into a skip. Well, I'd always wanted to be a fireman, and now I had my chance. By the time the fire brigade arrived I had the fire under control but was still going berserk with the hosepipe, causing more damage with the water I'd squirted everywhere than the actual fire had done.

Another time a prison inmate came to be married and I was asked to keep lookout, together with a police officer. While the ceremony was being conducted three scruffy-looking men came to the front door and asked where the wedding was. I let them in through the back into the room where the prisoner was waiting with two warders. The next minute I heard a scuffle break out. The men knocked out the warders and took their keys, then made their escape through the windows and across a field. I never heard whether the prisoner was recaptured or not.

Working alone a lot of the time could be a bit dodgy too. One time I was patrolling the building and I came across a strange-looking man in the records department. I asked him what he was doing there and he said,

'I'm just admiring the architecture,' and started to rub his hands over the walls. He said, 'You know, I'm an educated man. I went to Eton and I also played cricket.' As he talked he mimed the acts of writing, playing cricket and rugger. Then he said, 'I was good at boxing too,' and with that he punched me on the chin and did a runner as I fell to my knees. I pressed the panic button, and my colleague Colin Jackson grabbed him at the top of the stairs before calling the police.

These were highlights in an otherwise pretty boring job, and eventually I was moved once again to the registry office switchboard. It felt as if I was destined to be a switchboard operator for the rest of my life.

Like every teenager I had some tough lessons to learn about growing up, learning to work with adults and entering their world. Although I had lots of friends who were girls I rarely got further than that with them, but I still wasn't too bothered. All my spare time was taken up with football and, at eighteen, I retook my FA coaching badge. Again I passed with flying colours, but this time without having to lie about my age.

I tried to treat the family when I could. I was so grateful for all they – my mum, my Nan and Granddad Skyner – had done for me. We'd never been able to afford a colour telly but I'd enjoyed nights with my granddad, watching the footy on the black-and-white set. He'd have a pint of his home brew, and he'd dip a glass in it and give some to me when my mum wasn't looking.

I went down to Rumbelows in town and bought a fourteen-inch colour telly out of my allowance. It sounds rubbish now, but it was state-of-the-art then. They were going to deliver it between ten and twelve on the Saturday morning. Well, on Saturday mornings we always went down to St John's Market to buy nuts from the Nut Centre and pigs' feet and belly pork from the butchers' stalls, which Mum would boil up for a weekend treat. It got to eleven o'clock. I was like a cat on a hot tin roof and I kept delaying them and my granddad said,

'Come on, Gary. We have to go,' and I kept saying,

'Oh, not yet,' and I kept going to the toilet, till they said,

'What's wrong with you this morning?'

Anyway, at last there was a ring at the door, and they were all gobsmacked when the telly was brought in.

'What did you do that for?' they said, but they were thrilled to bits. And it was great after that, sitting watching the footy with Pa.

I've always tried to share what I have. I've never used the money as a weapon against my family although I know some thalidomiders have, coercing family members into doing what they want. Luckily for me, there weren't any of those problems with my own family.

Handling money was another thing I had to learn as a young man, more so than many other young men of a similar age and class as myself in those days. I had thalidomide mates whose friends and relations would appear like magic when the annual payments were due, and they would feel obliged to kit them out in the latest gear and buy presents for the kids. And because you know you have some money, and they haven't, you do feel obliged. I always feel I have to pay for anything anyone does for me, especially when they are not family. It's difficult for me to accept that some people want to do things for you out of affection or respect.

I did waste a lot of money, as young people do, on clothes and on pissing it up against the wall. But I also tried to be generous, especially with my family. On the other hand, I wouldn't let myself be taken for a mug. One Christmas I was about twenty-one. By then I'd come into my money from the Trust, so I suppose I was quite well off (compared to other people of my age). My sister Karen was about eighteen or nineteen. Her friend Linda had been thrown out of her family's home and she was staying with us. They both worked behind the bar in a local pub and I said to them,

'What do you want for Christmas?' and they came out with a big list of stuff, and I thought, *God, they think I've got a few bob.* Soft-arse me went out and got what they wanted and they said,

'Well, what do you want?' I said I could do with a radio for the car and they went,

'Oh, we'll club together and get you that: a cassette radio.' Christmas Day came and they said, 'Oh, Halfords haven't got them in yet, but they're coming in on Boxing Day so we'll pick it up then.'

So I said, 'OK.' On New Year's Eve there was still no sign of it and I asked, 'Any news on the radio?' and they said,

'Oh, yeah… January sales, they're coming in.'

On 22 February I started to think I'd been had off so I said to my mum,

'They're taking the piss out of me,' and she said,

'Oh, leave them alone. They haven't got any money. You've got a few bob. You've got a good job, and they're only working behind the bar.'

I said, 'Hang on. They asked me what I wanted and I told them, so they should have got it. If they couldn't afford it they should have said so.'

Pubs used to shut at three in the afternoon in those days, and the two of them were walking back up the hill from work one day when I was driving past. It was pouring with rain and they were under a brolly and I pulled the car up and said,

'Get in… get in,' and they went,

'Ah, thanks.' They got in and I drove down the road and turned off into Aigburth Road and they said, 'You've missed our turning,' and I said,

'No, I haven't,' and I went right down to Otterspool Prom. I parked there and said, 'Leave your brollies and coats and get out of the car.'

They went, 'What?' and I said, 'Get out of the car now. Yous two think I'm fucking daft. Out, and leave your purses,' so they couldn't get a taxi back. The two of them were just in skirts and blouses, and it was hammering down. I know it was a bastard of a thing to do but I left them and drove home and my mum said,

'Our Karen's late… you know, coming back from work.' I just sat watching the wrestling on the telly while Mum was making my tea and I said,

'Oh, she's probably gabbing. You know what she's like.'

The next thing it was bang, bang on the door, and the two of them were standing there like drowned rats, shouting,

'He's fucking crackers,' and, 'He's fucking nuts… evil bastard.'

My mum said, 'Gary Skyner, you didn't do that to them, did you?'

I said,' It was either that or I threw them in the Mersey. The two of you have had me off.'

They laughed about it later, but my mother went berserk. But that'll give you an idea of what I am like. It wasn't the fact that they didn't buy me the present, it was that they thought they could take me for a ride. That's how I am. Life has taught me never to let anyone get one over on me.

Me and Karen with our pet dog Ringo

In any case, Karen and I fought like cat and dog. Although I was happy living at home, she and I were both teenagers with teenagers' unstable emotions. At times they spilled over into physical violence. She'd hit me on the head with the wooden clogs that were in fashion then, or anything that came to hand. Once she stabbed me with a fork, and on one occasion I shot her in the leg with an air rifle. Was it all part of a normal family upbringing? I don't know, but that tension has always been there between us.

Despite all that, she's still my sister. Years later she got toxaemia when she was pregnant, and her life hung by a thread. I remember grabbing the doctor and telling him,

'If she dies, you die as well.' My mum went mad, but deep down there is that brother-sister bond. It's just that... put us together and we fight like fuck.

Much as I've always adored my mum, there was tension there as well. She was very bitter about my dad for years after he left. I tried to defend him and justify what he did (God knows why). I suppose I still had that idea that men should stick together and had the concept of the ideal father-son bond in my head… which, in our case, in reality, just didn't exist.

Mum was always attacking my idealised picture and my defence of him. She would get really angry, saying,

'When are you going to wake up to him?' She could be so hurtful, and sometimes I thought that bitterness had skewed her vision and was turning her into one of those poisonous divorcees – the woman scorned.

In the end I had to face up to the callous way he had treated us. I could excuse his horror at my deformity and his feelings of shame at having produced me, but he'd lived with me all those years and seen how I'd fought to overcome the obstacles he thought I could never overcome. In my mind he'd denigrated the way my mum had fought to make a family life for us all with love and hard work by just going off and leaving us. It forced me at last to accept the lack of love. I saw clearly that my dreams of a good relationship with him were just pie in the sky.

I can't forgive him for the bitter hurt that left its mark on both me and my mum. These things create a legacy, a burden you can't rid yourself of. Every time I struggle to achieve something I find that each success brings hard memories of his words and his expression. He said,

'You'll never be able to do that,' about so many things. The sneers and the rejection always raise multiple heads at each moment of achievement.

On the other hand, maybe I have spent my whole life trying to impress him and rid myself of these demons by taking on ever higher challenges. Maybe I would never have done half the things I have done if he hadn't been so critical, so perhaps I should thank him for that. Would I have been happier if things had been different, if I'd led a quieter life? Or is my nature such that I would be bored by the everyday? Who knows?

I was certainly bored with working as a switchboard

operator. My next job was a complete and welcome change. It was training to be a welder. I'd been moaning to my mate John Smith about my boring job and he promised to speak to his dad, who owned a welding company, to see if he could get me on there. Good enough, John Smith Sr. took me on as an apprentice, and I went to work at the firm in Brasenose Road, Bootle. John Smith Sr. was a bit of an inventor, and he made all sorts of aids for me to enable me to use the welding equipment.

Now I wore a boiler suit, and I felt like a working man – and proud of it. I went through several boiler suits, however, as I was always setting fire to myself. But, luckily, I survived my training. I loved my time there. My mate John Jr. taught me different types of welding: gas-electric, argon welding, etc., and John Sr. brought in a tutor for me who adapted a crutch and pliers for me so I could control the welding rods. As always, I was determined to succeed despite my physical limitations.

It was great to be working with a gang of lads, and we had some fun times. One time, when I hadn't been there long, we were working away in Holyhead and we were staying in digs. Two of the lads thought they would give me an initiation and crept up on me in the middle of the night, putting a hand over my mouth. Thinking someone was trying to molest me I leapt up, butted one and kicked the other. Then I fled out on to the balcony with my mattress, where I spent the rest of the night. We all had a good laugh about it in the morning.

Another time we were working in Ford's, and lots of batteries were going missing from the site. The police were called in and they thought it was us. We knew who it was, but we wouldn't say anything. One night I got stopped in my car on the way home and the coppers asked me what was in the boot so I told them it was footy kit and stuff. They asked me the registration number and I told them.

'You remembered that well,' was the comment, and I said, 'What do you mean?' and the cop said,

'Your name's Gary Skyner?'

I said, 'Yes.' He said, 'This car's not registered to you. It's registered to the Thalidomide Children's Trust.'

At that I held up my arms and said,

'Where do you think I got these from, the fucking Wizard's Den?' (This was a joke shop in Moorfields at that time). The cop pissed himself laughing, and told me to fuck off.

One of the receptionists at the firm had a really sexy telephone voice, but physically she was very ugly. She'd get good orders from the reps on the phone because she sounded so attractive, and because all the men pictured a smouldering blonde or brunette. She got loads of offers of lunch dates, and we would wait to see them approach the window then recoil as she drew back the frosted glass. It was a good laugh to see their faces, and we knew that the promised expensive lunch at a fancy restaurant would be downgraded to a pie and a pint in the local pub.

Fate took a hand just when things seemed to be going well. Another catastrophe befell me when my beloved granddad Pa Skyner died in 1980. He was struck down with cancer, and died on 13th October at six minutes past eleven.

My mum was heartbroken, as he had always treated her as if she was his own daughter, but I was completely devastated. On the day of the funeral my dad called to say that he and his new wife Marge would be occupying the first car in the funeral cortège, and that my mum would have to travel in the second car. All my grief rose up in a burst of anger and I jumped into my car and drove at breakneck speed to my dad's place, which was seven miles away. As soon as I got there I ran at him and pinned him down on the floor. I think I would have killed him if my Uncle Arthur hadn't pleaded with me to stop, saying there was already enough grief and reminding me of the solemnity of the occasion. I calmed down a bit when he went on to side with me and castigated my dad for putting Marge in front of my mum.

The United Welding football team with
all three League cups.

It wasn't long after that when they emigrated to Australia, and I was glad to see them go. My mum's parents had been dead for some time (Grandma Ellis passed away in 1966 and Granddad Ellis in 1968), but losing Pa Skyner left a terrible hole in my life. Luckily I had many friends, a good job and my football to give me some consolation.

One of the best things about working at United Welding was the football team. While I was there we won the Liverpool Business League minor, junior and senior cups, not just in one year but in three consecutive years (1981–2, 1982–3 and 1983–84). This was a feat no one else had achieved in the League's eighty-year history.

Unfortunately all good things come to an end and there are some difficulties that you can't surmount, no matter how determined you are. I'd done two years at United Welding when trouble came in the shape of a mysterious lung complaint that eventually put me in hospital. My X-ray results showed inflammation caused by fume inhalation. The hospital doctor told me in no uncertain terms that, if I didn't pack the job in, I would be dead before my twenty-fifth birthday.

I was gutted. I'd really enjoyed working with my hands. I'd felt I was doing something creative and worthwhile, as well as being part of a great team. John's dad kept me on at the firm but, once again, I found myself operating a switchboard. It wasn't the same, and after a while I left there and went to work at the Liverpool City Engineers' Department. I was still on the switchboard there and my job was to inform drivers and technical staff of details of outgoing jobs, such as fallen trees or collapsed buildings. My area was Liverpool's Breckside Park, and I was engaged on a six-month contract.

One of the conditions of my contract was that I didn't take any time off during the six months. I had a holiday booked to Ibiza, but I didn't worry too much about it. I thought once I'd got settled into the job that, with my gift of the gab, I'd be able to talk my boss into letting me go.

When the time came I thought about taking sick leave. It wouldn't have been a problem for me to get a doctor's note for a fortnight, but then I don't like swinging the lead and I thought I might have problems explaining away a Mediterranean tan. So I came clean and asked if I could take unpaid leave. As I expected, the boss said,

'No problem. Go with my blessing.'

I was amazed when I rang home while I was in Ibiza and my mum told me that a letter had come from work telling me I was sacked. I was fuming, and as soon as I got home I prepared for a showdown. I took my mate Jimmy Coulthard with me. Jimmy was well known as a hard man in Liverpool. He worked as a doorman in the city's pubs and clubs. He was a gentle giant, really, but a bit of an animal if crossed.

Well, when we walked in the office my boss did a disappearing trick so we decided to go to the top, and we went down town to the main council office and marched into Derek Hatton's room. No one tried to stop us. I said,

'Listen, you—' I didn't know who he was then. I told him what happened and I said, 'If you don't do something—', and I started throwing a few names out of people I knew. He kept saying,

'I know him, and I know him…' so it seemed as if we had a few things in common. After a while he said, 'You're really mad over this, aren't you?'

I said, 'Mad? If I'd got hold of my boss I'd have fucking killed him.'

'OK,' he said. 'Leave it with me. I'll see what I can do.' Then Jimmy had to stick his oar in and say,

'Don't fuck him about or I'll throw you out the window.'

I was trying to shut him up, going, 'Not now, Jimmy. Fucking hell, we're getting somewhere now.'

Anyway, he was true to his word and got me back in the council, but not in the same job. Instead I was placed in the messenger service at City Estates. Derek and I were to become quite pally later, when I worked in the housing department and he was on the housing committee.

Me with Derek Hatton (centre) and boxer Paul Hodkinson (right) in 1994.

I worked at the messenger service for two years. It wasn't the most exciting of jobs. It involved delivering internal mail throughout various council departments but it set me up as a council employee, and that made it easier for me to apply for other jobs in the council.

My next job was as assistant housing manager at Belle Vale housing office. I got on well there with my boss Steve Gow and the assistant manager, John Kirkham. Like me, they were Liverpool supporters and we shared the same sense of humour.

You really needed it in that job. It was a far cry from trotting round filling pigeonholes with mail. There were some hilarious and some hair-raising moments as well as some sad ones. Perhaps the saddest one was when we got a call out to a home where we found two dead dogs, and they had been dead for over a month. The smell was unbelievable, and the lady tenant had obviously been having problems for some time. There were dog turds everywhere, and she'd actually decorated the place and painted over some of them with white gloss paint.

I never thought that having the power to allocate tenancies might put me at risk, but I soon learnt otherwise. I had people coming in – sometimes on a daily basis – hoping to cajole, threaten or coerce their way to a tenancy. One man, I remember, told me that if I didn't give him a flat he would be waiting for me outside when I left work. This was another occasion when I was glad of my club doorman friends. I made a few phone calls, and when I walked out of the office three of my pals were waiting. They grabbed the man before he could accost me.

The housing office was built on top of Belle Vale Shopping Centre and had its own rooftop car park. This bloke found himself dangling by the ankles over the edge. My mates told him in no uncertain terms,

'Come here again, threatening Gary, and we'll drop you off.'

The so-called gentle sex could be just as bad, if not worse. One lady who desperately wanted a transfer kept coming in every day badgering for a change of tenancy. In the end I took her in a private room to be interviewed. Suddenly she said,

'I know I'm getting a move today.'

'What makes you think that?' I asked.

She had this big shopping bag and she said,

'Because of this,' and whipped out a gallon can of petrol and a lighter.

Not stopping to think, I jumped up and kicked the table. It knocked her down and fell on top of her and she dropped the can, which sprayed petrol everywhere. We were rolling about in it with me trying to grab the lighter. It was like a scene from an action movie. Suddenly one of the housing assistants, Ian Fazakerly, burst into the room, and together we managed to restrain her.

My clothes were covered in petrol, and I was still stinking of it when I got home. My mum said,

'What kind of job is that where people are prepared to kill you to get a flat?' Sometimes I found myself asking the same question.

There were certainly some strange characters in the area I covered. This area included The Hawthorns, which were the name of two of the high-rise blocks so beloved of 1960s city planners and architects. This type of housing was seen as the solution to inner-city overcrowding at the time, along with new towns like Skelmersdale and suburban estates like Speke and Croxteth. Many people from the old terraced streets off Lodge Lane were housed in The Hawthorns, and when they were first built they were seen as very desirable, state-of-the-art properties. The sad history of high-rise flats is well documented. Those who live in them now are often the most disadvantaged, who have few choices.

When I worked in Belle Vale, The Hawthorns were already becoming notorious for theft and drug problems and, as in all council estates, good law-abiding citizens were driven to distraction by the bad apples.

An old lady living in the flats reported a tenant on the top floor who kept throwing things out of the windows. These were not small items, but stuff like washing machines and other appliances. She produced a photo she'd taken of the tenant, who was half-naked and wielding a baseball bat. A colleague and I paid him a visit and he received us politely, even offering us tea and biscuits. He seemed perfectly normal, and nothing like the man in the photo. We could do no more than warn him about his behaviour and leave.

A few weeks later we got a call from the police to say that a man was running amok at The Hawthorns and they had sent officers out. When we arrived at the scene with a police escort we found it was the same man, but now he was going berserk with a baseball bat. He ran at us and was only stopped by one of the policemen, who knocked him unconscious with his truncheon. I thought back to the afternoon we'd gone into his flat without protection, and thanked my lucky stars he'd been in a quiet phase that day.

Working at Belle Vale was certainly a risky business, but once I'd shown I wouldn't be easily frightened and that I had tough mates (who were tougher than the scallies who thought they'd have a go at me) I was shown some respect and didn't have much trouble.

It wasn't just at work, though. I was quite well known in the local pubs. One night I was drinking in the Aigburth Arms with a mate, Norman Weaver, when an argument broke out between the licensee, David Kelly and a couple of yobbos. The pair took a look at us and obviously thought I, at least, posed no threat, before launching a vicious attack on the landlord. Boy, were they in for a shock. Norman and I waded in to the rescue, and my footy skills came in handy as I floored them both with my feet. Following their arrest and conviction I received a letter of appreciation from the chief constable of Merseyside Police, which I treasure to this day.

I like to think that in my job I had a reputation for fair dealing, and would try to help those in most need. However, trouble continued at The Hawthorns. There were a number of pensioners living there, and their lives were made a misery by some of the other tenants. They were forever complaining about the hooliganism, and nothing ever seemed to get done about it.

One Friday afternoon, after we had closed up and were preparing to go home for the weekend, there was a knock at the door. I went to the spyhole and there was an old dear outside, plaintively asking to see the manager on an urgent matter. I felt sorry for her so I opened the door and another twenty or so pensioners rushed in... followed by Derek Hatton, who was then councillor for Belle Vale. They'd all brought flasks and sandwiches and were obviously prepared for a sit-in, organised by the politically aware Derek. An ultimatum was issued that they weren't moving until we did something about their plight. Instead of my usual Friday night out my colleagues and I spent most of the evening at the police station, as all the women were arrested for public order offences.

It was certainly a sensational tactic. Derek Hatton was then on the housing committee and could probably have solved the problem internally, but it was a recurring difficulty involving many people. It really required a shift in housing policy away from mixing young and elderly tenants in the same building, so that elderly people weren't plagued by loud music, drug dealing and nutcases. Nobody seemed able to intervene so Derek probably felt that the best thing was to get them all together in protest. On the other hand, councillors always have an eye on potential votes and tend to embrace any publicity that enhances their reputation in the eyes of the voters.

My days at Belle Vale were, overall, happy ones, but major life changes were in store for me. In 1985 my Grandma Skyner died, and it was really the end of my relationship with my dad. By then he and Marge were living in Australia, but I was sickened that he didn't make the effort to come to the funeral. After that I only really called when there was a family emergency. But even then he never came to the phone, and I had to relay messages through Marge.

I can't help feeling that he was heavily influenced by her. Despite our differences I don't believe he would have behaved this way if he hadn't been with Marge. And it wasn't just me. He was the same with Karen and with other family members. I think Marge always felt unsure of him and urged him to forget about us. We were to be just part of the past. It seemed that he wanted to sever all ties with the family. Well, so be it.

On a happier note, two things happened that would open up a whole new world for me. One was my entry into the world of stand-up comedy. The other was meeting Shelagh, the girl who would become my wife.

Chapter 7

A Funny Thing Happened to Me...

I'd always been the class clown at school, and when I grew up I transferred to being the pub joker. All my life I've been accustomed to being the centre of attention, for both good and bad reasons. I guess I learned to deal with it and to turn it to my advantage at an early age.

Even in primary school I developed the ability to give as good as I got to those who skitted me and I turned the tables by making myself popular through humour and telling jokes. So it wasn't long before I was entertaining the regulars at my local during after-hours stay-behinds or lockouts, as we called them. People began saying to me that I should think about getting paid for what I was doing.

My first stage appearance was at the United Services Club, and all my mates from the Aigburth Arms turned out to see me. Unfortunately I had yet to learn the art of gauging the audience. It didn't dawn on me that the large number of elderly people in the audience wouldn't appreciate my liberal use of four-letter words, and I was dismayed when a few of them complained. A couple of my mates consoled me, saying,

'Come on, Gary, you've got talent. You just need to get a proper act together.' I took their advice and worked hard to create a professional routine.

I was asked to perform at the Ball of Ditton, near Widnes in Cheshire. It was a Sunday afternoon charity do and I got paid £200. I couldn't believe I was getting so much for doing something I enjoyed, and the show went really well. The next week I was asked to do another charity show in Kirkby. This one only paid £50 but that was still good money in 1986, and again I went down really well.

An early promotional shot of me

After that I looked round for charity shows anywhere in my local area, and soon gained a reputation as a very funny bloke. It's maybe got to do with how much I enjoy being in the spotlight. Some people get nervous before they go on stage, but not me. Like I said, I'm used to being stared at, and it's so much better when they're listening to you and laughing with you rather than gawking at your disability. Maybe I'm just an egotistical maniac. I love being patted on the back and told how good I am.

Perhaps too, I enjoyed the culture and the excitement

of the nightlife. As always in my life there were some hairy moments. May 1986 saw me convicted for drunk driving, but my experience at the hands of the police that night was a memorable one.

I'd been auditioning in Birmingham for the TV talent show *New Faces*. I felt the auditions had gone well so on my return I called a few mates, and we did a tour of South Liverpool's pubs before ending up in a nightclub. We came out about 2 am, got in my red Ford Orion and drove off.

That night four lads had stolen a car and had spent the evening baiting the police, which had instigated a major police chase. You can guess what make and model of car they had stolen. As I drove through Toxteth my mate Jimmy said we'd just passed a bizzy van (a police van), so I put my foot down and headed for Jimmy's house. Suddenly we were surrounded by police cars coming at us from all directions.

I turned into Jimmy's street, only then remembering it was a dead end. My options weren't great: leg it down the railway line, or jump into the Mersey and swim for it. Even though I was pissed I realised these weren't viable solutions so I turned out the lights and Jimmy and I ducked down, hoping we had lost the cops.

Fat chance. The street lit up like Blackpool Illuminations as it filled with police cars shining their roof lights on us. Two officers approached the car. One began inspecting the car. The other came to the window and asked,

'Are you the driver of this vehicle?' Even in the state I was in, or perhaps because of it, I couldn't pass up the opportunity for a joke.

'Well, it's automatic, but I have to be here.'

'Do you know why you've been stopped?'

'No. I'm a comic, not a clairvoyant.'

'Have you been drinking, sir?'

'I might have had a couple, officer.'

'I have a bag here that will tell us if you're drunk.'

'Snap. I've got one at home that does the same.'

'Will you step out of the car, sir?'

Clearly he didn't appreciate my sense of humour, as no sooner had I got out of the car than there was a whack, a thump and a smack. Reeling, I said,

'Hang on. I know I take the piss out of you lads, but there's no need for this.'

That only annoyed him further, as another rain of blows landed on me. I could hear Jimmy protesting to the other copper that I was a thalidomider and that the car was legit. That put a stop to the violence, but it didn't save me from being nicked. Once they'd calmed down, checked the car – and found we were telling the truth – I guess they saved face by doing me for drink-driving. There wasn't any doubt about that, as back at the station the breathalyser registered 50 mg over 35 mg.

After being locked in a cell for some time and being deprived of socks and shoes (and with no blanket or anything), I was finally released, and later received a £50 fine and a twelve–month driving ban. I thought about pursuing a charge of assault on the officer who had beaten me up but in the end decided not to. I'd always felt reasonably supportive of the police force and I figured that this time I'd been in the wrong, and had perhaps provoked the officer by being a smart alec.

However, not long after, something else happened that permanently altered my feelings about our police. I had a long-term booking at Cassinelli's club near Wigan, and one particular night several tables had been booked by police officers from the same station I'd been booked at for the drink-driving incident. At this time I'd recently started going out with Shelagh, who would become my wife, and news had got back to me that the officer who'd assaulted me on the night of the car chase had been trying to get off with Shelagh and kept getting the knock-back. Apparently his officer mates had been skitting him, saying that Gary Skyner could not only outdrive him but could pull the girls better.

I went on stage expecting some heckling from this bloke, but it got far worse than that. As I went on with my routine this guy climbed on his table and announced to the audience that I was a drink-driver, and shouted out all the details of my conviction. He and other officers from the division completely disrupted my show, and I couldn't let that pass.

I lodged a complaint with the Liverpool Police Authority and was asked to come to the Merseyside Police headquarters, where a senior official asked me to drop the charges with a promise that he would deal with it personally and I would have no further trouble. I consulted my solicitor, Kevin Dooley, and his response was,

'There are 4,800 of them, and only one of you.' I signed the agreement not to press charges and, fair play, there have been no incidents of harassment since.

Comedy began to overtake my other interests. At the time I was still managing the United Welding football team even though I no longer worked there, but football seemed to be generating a lot of bad feeling so when a referee's car was vandalised I started to think it was time to quit. Anyhow, around that time I started going out with Shelagh, and between courting and comedy there wasn't much time for football.

I hadn't had many real girlfriends but I wasn't a complete innocent, either. My first full sexual experience came when I was twenty-three. That may sound incredibly late – but hey-ho, it's not so easy for someone like me. That first girl's name was Barbara, and we met in a pub in Woolton. I wasn't expecting anything, least of all to get lucky, but I gave her a load of guff about my mum being away on holiday and me having to go back to her house to put the lights on… and, to my surprise, Barbara agreed to come with me for a coffee.

So we went to my mum's house, had a coffee and she just said,

'Oh, well… we're both adults, aren't we? So let's just go to bed,' and I thought, *There you go. Start the car.*

The funny thing was that when my mum got back from Torquay I got this barrage of abuse. She said,

'I'll fucking kill you. What have you been doing in my bed?'

I thought *Oh, shit. I forgot to clear up.* But, you know… twenty-three years old and getting bollocked for that. I've never forgotten that. Next time I went round to Mum's I expected to get it in the neck again but she just started laughing and said,

'You're a fucking case you,' and I was thinking *No, you're a case for thinking that I wouldn't.*

I suppose I did miss out a bit on the lifestyle of other young blokes of my age who were chopping and changing girlfriends and then getting married, but I had quite a lot of girlfriends who I went out with even though there might be no real sexual relationship there. And there were times when I struck incredibly lucky. There was this beautiful girl who used to come in the pub. She was the spit of Debbie Harry, and when she walked in all the lads would look up. She had this really good-looking fella too. They made kind of the perfect couple, and they both knew it – you know, the kind who love themselves – but every guy in the pub would have given his right hand to sleep with her.

Somehow, one Monday night, after we'd been training, my mate Jimmy and me ended up drinking with her and her mate. We got on really well and I tried to get a late stay-behind from the pub manager but he wasn't having it, and offered me a couple of bottles of wine instead. At that time I was living in a house in Grassington Crescent and I thought, *You're pissing in the wind. There's no chance she's going to go home with you*. So I went back to the table with the wine and she said,

'Oh, did you get that so we could have a drink?'

I said, 'Yes, me and Jimmy are going back to the house, but you won't want to come.' She said, 'No, no, we'll come back with you,' and when we got back it happened. Although outwardly I may appear very confident... honestly, I'm not when it comes to women, and all the time it was going on I couldn't believe it was real. Nobody in their wildest dreams would have believed it, least of all me.

The next Saturday we were all in the pub as usual and she came in with her fella. It was hilarious, really, because all the lads were eyeing her up and saying,

'Oh, I'd give her one,' and all that, and I was saying,

'No fucking chance there.'

It just shows how unconfident I was, because of my arms and that. I'd never dream of going for someone flamboyant like that. I'd be too scared of getting knocked back – and yet, out of the blue, it happened. It just goes to show that beauty isn't in the eye of the beholder, I suppose.

Anyway, so I wasn't completely innocent when Shelagh came along, but I wasn't really expecting a serious relationship. It just seemed to happen, and it was Shelagh who made the running. From what I discovered later, she came after me and she got me.

We already knew each other as I knew her sister Maria, who would come in my local. Maria was always going on about Shelagh, and how her dad favoured Shelagh over her. She kept showing me photos of her and I thought nothing of it, but then she said she would bring her to meet me as she thought we would get on well.

I did ask Shelagh out a couple of times but she turned me down, saying that her dad didn't like her going out with older men. I thought she was just putting me off without being rude. She was usually with her mate Lindsey and Lindsey only liked men in uniform, so I thought Shelagh must be the same.

In 1986 Maria was going out with Ian Webb, one of my childhood friends. I'd seen Shelagh in the Cabin Club in town a few times, and even given her a lift home once or twice. At that time I had a couple of casual girlfriends, but nothing serious.

One night Shelagh was in a cab going home after a night out with one of her friends, Marie Berry, when she started crying. Marie asked what was wrong and Shelagh said she was sick of men because the bloke she'd danced with hadn't asked her out again. She said she'd never get the one she really wanted. Marie said,

'Who's that then?' and she said,

'He wouldn't look at me twice. He's got two girlfriends already. It's Gary Skyner.'

Marie said, 'Where does he drink? We'll go there on Saturday.'

The next thing the two of them came in the pub, and that's how it started.

Within a year we were married at Sefton Park Unitarian Church. Some people thought we were like chalk and cheese. I remember one of my mates trying to talk me out of the marriage, saying that we didn't match up and I was only getting married because I was scared of being left on the shelf. Shelagh had quite a timid personality compared to my rumbustious, outgoing nature, so I suppose we did make a bit of a strange pair.

Other people thought it strange too. My mum was in the hairdresser's one time, and met up with an old family friend who'd just returned from living in South Africa for many years. She was surprised to learn that I was married, and asked my mum who the lucky lady was. When told it was Shelagh, she went,

'Shiggy? That timid little girl married Gary? I can't believe it. She must have changed radically.'

Cutting the cake at our wedding.

Nevertheless, married we were. And we stayed married for almost thirty years, with our relationship cemented by our two lovely daughters. Of course there were both love and tears and, on looking back now, I can see that we each had needs that the other fulfilled. In my case I needed someone to love and care for me, and maybe part of it was that Shelagh was attracted by the security I could provide. Like most marriages there were good and bad times, and we had some very turbulent spots. Shelagh has always been a home bird and, as my comedy role developed, more and more often I kept unsociable hours or was away from home altogether.

In 1987 I entered the Whitbread All Merseyside Talent Competition, which was held at the Montrose Club. I won all the heats and the grand final. The prize was £1,000 and a holiday in Tenerife. I was elated.

The manager at the Montrose was Ernie Mac and he became my first manager, giving me the chance to perform to large audiences of 400 plus. He had another club called The 29 Club and he introduced me to many famous comics, including Ken Dodd, Hal Nolan, Stan Boardman and Eddie Flanagan. Of course Liverpool is famous for its comedy stars. In fact it's often said that you have to be a comedian to live in Liverpool, and I guess that's true.

Eddie Flanagan was one of my heroes in the comedy world. When I was younger I'd always make sure I watched *The Comedians*, a TV show featuring stand-up comics, when he was on. Little did I know then that Eddie would become a friend and an advisor. I learned so much from this great man, and if he had lived longer maybe he would have become my manager or professional advisor. A fitting epitaph to this comedy genius is a joke he used to tell:

'Two plumbers meet on the street. One says,
"Did you hear Eddie died last night?"
The other says, "Ah, God bless him, when's the funeral?"
'Two comics meet on the street. One says,
"Did you hear Eddie died last night?"
The other says, "No, which club was he on?"'
Anyway, my own comedy career started to expand rapidly,

and it became clear that Ernie Mac had too much work on his hands looking after his clubs to manage me properly. I'm eternally grateful to Ernie for giving me my start, but it was time to move on.

Early days: a prized photo with Bruce Grobbelaar.

Les Bather was my next manager. He lived with his wife in a flat over a betting shop in Garston and his front room was his office (so you can imagine he was a fairly small-time operator), but he got me into talent shows and on to local radio. I did spots with the local celebrity presenters: Billy Butler and Wally Scott on Radio Merseyside, and Phil Easton and Johnny Kennedy on Radio City.

It was all good exposure but I soon realised I wasn't going to go much further with Les. I needed more bookings and better connections. I had stars in my eyes. In the end Les told me to go for one of the agents in the north-east. He gave me a list of phone numbers, adding dryly,

'If you can make Geordies laugh you can make anyone laugh.'

I'd already begun to move beyond the Liverpool scene, and I'd taken a few bookings from a female promoter from Bolton. Her name was Crystal, and she became my agent for a while. She specialised in stag shows and the raunchier side of comedy, taking bookings for strippers as well as comics. I could cope with all that but stag dos and that kind of thing can get pretty wild, and sometimes I found myself in the firing line.

Nowadays lap dancing clubs have taken over, but in those days it was all strip shows. After the girls had done a couple of routines a bucket would go round to get money for them to do a full-on lesbian routine. As comic I would have the mic, and it would fall to me to negotiate the price with the girls and to get the punters to put enough cash in the bucket. I'd have to go out front and say how much the girls wanted before they'd come back out.

At one club I worked there was a stripper called Helga. She used to be a tank driver, and she came from Ukraine. She used to be amazed at all the stuff you could buy in the shops here because, I suppose, there wasn't much around where she came from. She never missed an opportunity for a good scoff, and as soon as she arrived she would ask for a plate from the buffet before she would do her routine. One night she asked for food and the manager said,

'There's no buffet tonight. It's hotpot.'

'What is hotpot?' asked Helga. When it was explained to her she said,

'Bring me dish,' and she proceeded to fill up a bowl with the hotpot, which she then wrapped in cling film and put in her enormous handbag to take home for her supper.

On another night she was asked to do a live show for the lads after her strip routine, and she said to me,

'I want £100. Nothing less.'

I went out with the bucket and told the lads to cough up,

but they were all putting in 50p pieces and the like. I came back and said to Helga,

'Doesn't look like a hundred nicker in there.'

She tipped it all out on the floor and got down on her hands and knees to count it. Eventually she sat back and looked at me.

'It comes to £39.50,' she said. 'It will do.' I guess she'd learnt how to make the best of things in this world.

I got used to the girls who worked the clubs, and I got used to women parading around in the nude. One night I took my mate George with me to a club called Jaguars in Coventry. We were in the dressing room when this girl came in stark naked after finishing her act, and started giving me a load of grief about how terrible the audience was and about some bloke at the front who kept trying to pinch her arse.

There weren't any toilet facilities backstage, and the next thing she did was to cock her leg up and piss in the sink while still carrying on her conversation with me. I heard a sort of gasp and looked round, and saw that George was absolutely gobsmacked.

'What's up, mate?' I asked. It just didn't dawn on me, because I was so used to seeing naked women. I got to know a bit about some of the girls in our backstage chats, and a lot of them were just young mums trying to make a few extra bob.

One night I was doing this pub in Burnley when it got raided. I ran upstairs and hid in a wardrobe in the private quarters. After a while, when all the noise had died down, I cautiously cracked open the door. The door swung open with a squeaking noise – eeeeee – and this copper was sitting there on the end of the bed. He said,

'I saw you going upstairs and I knew you must either be in the wardrobe or in the bathroom but I didn't want to run into the bathroom in case you were on the toilet, so I thought I'd just sit here and wait.'

I thought, *Well I'm fucked now. How can I explain being in a wardrobe full of clothes?* He said, 'You know this will be all over the newspapers. You've got enough problems already. Just fuck off.'

I said, 'It's nothing to do with me, anyway. I'm only a punter,' but he wasn't having that.

He said, 'What? Wearing beach shorts and a tee shirt that says *Where's the beach?* in Burnley in the middle of winter? Go on, you tell a fine tale. Fuck off.' So he let me off.

There were a couple of venues in the Blackburn area where I was appearing on a regular basis. One was called The Red Parrot and the other was called The Rovers Return. Unlike its *Coronation Street* namesake this one had Sunday lunchtime shows, where I and two strippers entertained a male audience of around 700. I was quickly becoming quite well known.

Life could not only be wild, but sometimes downright dangerous. In those days comedy was very racist and sexist. Looking back on TV shows like *Love Thy Neighbour* and *The Benny Hill Show* now makes me cringe but we thought nothing of it then, and I have to admit that I told a lot of those kinds of jokes.

One night I had with me an ex-Olympic champion boxer, Brian Schumacher. I normally do a very good job of talking myself out of situations without needing any backup and I said,

'All I'm doing is giving you a few bob to carry my bags and stuff. Don't do anything unless I really need help.' I went down a bomb at the gig, but this Indian bloke came out afterwards and he said,

'You are very funny, but why do you do this material? It is very offensive to me.'

I said, 'I'm not being racist. It's just that it's funny.'

He said, 'No, no, I don't like it.'

So I was talking to him and doing a good job of calming him down, but the next thing this hand came over my shoulder and

Brian picked him up and slammed his head against the wall. Little did he know that the bloke had twenty of his family with him, and Brian was hitting them all. It was pandemonium. I opened the boot. I had a baseball bat in there and Brian was standing behind the boot and popping them all on the head. I was saying,

'Get in the car.' Anyway we got in the car and I said to him, 'Don't you ever do that again. We could have got fucking killed.' So that's how dodgy the game can be, but I do a good job on my own of backing my own corner and defusing possible trouble.

Thankfully attitudes to comedy have changed. It's not just a general social awareness that some things are unacceptable, but also a personal lesson that I have had to learn for myself. I used to tell a joke that involved a woman with a cleft palate. One night in Barrow I was telling this joke when a woman in the audience jumped up and started shouting,

'You bastard... you bastard.' Of course I didn't know she had a cleft palate, but it made me realise that what you say on stage has an effect on people and that some people will take what you say literally.

It's one thing when it's your own fault, but at times I've had to face the backlash from someone else's performance. At one of my many gigs with Ricky Tomlinson he got pretty political about Margaret Thatcher and the role of the police in the miners' strike. After the show he left before me, and he was probably halfway up the M4 when this woman came banging on the dressing room door. She shouted,

'Where the fuck is he, like? Where's that Tomlinson?'

I said, 'Oh, he's gone,'

She said, 'Aye, he will fucking go, if I get hold of him. My husband was a police officer and he was a gentleman, in uniform and out. To say that the police did this and that in the miners' strike...'

I was trying to play politician, I said, 'No, what Ricky meant was that Margaret Thatcher used the police as a means of crushing the miners. He wasn't saying the police, as individuals, were baddies. They were following instructions from Whitehall.'

'I don't give a fuck,' she said. 'He was saying the police were doing this and that and my husband was police and he was a gentleman,' and she went on and on. The next morning I went to have a cup of tea with Ricky and I said to him,

'I could have killed you last night, the amount of fucking earache I got over you.' Of course Ricky hadn't meant to target anyone, and if he'd still been there when the woman came backstage he'd have been the first to apologise. But it's a fact that when you are frequently in the public eye you can't avoid upsetting someone now and again, no matter how hard you try to be diplomatic.

King of Comedy, that's me.

However, these were minor distractions in my rising status as an up-and-coming comedian. I won the title of Merseyside's King of Comedy for three consecutive years, in 1987, 1988 and 1989. While I was working round the Blackburn area an agent called Steve Draper phoned me and said he'd been in the audience at one of my shows and felt I had the potential to become a cabaret artist, which would be taking a step up from working the stag clubs.

Crystal, the agent who I'd been working with, wasn't very happy about me leaving to take up with Steve. But, although I was grateful for all she had done for me, I knew it was time to move on. My reputation was growing, and I needed someone who could get me bigger and better bookings. In 1989 I signed with Steve Draper, who was to be my manager for the next ten years.

Steve Draper was always very supportive and always tried to get me the best possible fee, and he stood up for me on those awful occasions in every comic's life when you die on stage. Fortunately there weren't very many of those. Soon I was working further afield, not only working the Lancashire/Merseyside area but being sent to bookings in the Midlands and further north, even into Scotland.

Although comedy work was building up I still remained in full-time employment with the council as the comedian's life is an uncertain one with no guaranteed income, and now I had a wife to look after and a home to pay for. I applied for and secured a Scale 4 post in the housing department, which gave me a higher salary. This job involved working in Liverpool's city centre in the Central Allocations Unit (CAU).

Going to work there was one of the worst mistakes I ever made. From the beginning the manager over me there made my life hell. At times I suffer with bowel problems, which is a common factor associated with thalidomide damage and it would necessitate me being off work sick, but this manager believed I was off because of my late nights doing comedy shows. It wasn't just him; the female supervisor and her assistant similarly had it in for me. They'd give me jobs to do that were physically difficult for me, like filing things on low shelves. At other times they would stop me going to the toilet during work time, saying I spent too much time in there. I felt I was being treated like a child, and there was no allowance made for my condition. I began to hate the job, but an opportunity arose for me to take revenge.

When Shelagh and I were first married we viewed a nice house and thought we'd put in an offer on it, but the estate agent told us someone else was interested. When she told us the name of the person I realised it was my supervisor from hell. Of course then I was determined to get the property at all costs, which I did. It gave me immense pleasure to go into work and give her my change of address details. I pretended not to know that she had been after the house and she never knew that I knew she had wanted it, but her face was a picture and I really enjoyed seeing that.

After that things just got worse. It wasn't just me. All the staff were terrified of my boss, but he seemed to go out of his way to pick on me. One day he crept up behind me, dropped a heap of files over my head and said,

'What's all this fucking shit? These letters are the biggest load of rubbish I have ever read. Do them all again.'

It was the straw that broke the camel's back. That afternoon I went to Derek Hatton's office and told him,

'If you don't get that bastard off my back I'll see to it myself.'

Derek hadn't forgotten the day I walked into his office with my bouncer friend Jimmy Coulthard, so he knew that my solution to the problem wouldn't end with us all taking tea together. He came over later that afternoon and had words with the manager, but it didn't really help and it was obvious that I couldn't carry on working there.

I got a transfer to the Garston housing department and at first I was much happier there, even though it had meant taking a drop in salary. The manager there, Don Baxter, was very welcoming and friendly, but soon it seemed that news of my problems at Central Allocations spread through the grapevine. Baxter obviously accepted the versions passed on by the CAU manager, and he too began to make things difficult for me. Again I was accused of swinging the lead when I was off sick.

I also think that because I was becoming something of a local celebrity there was some jealousy. Between working there and doing stand-up I was earning a good income, had a nice house and drove a big car. People would ring me at work for press quotes or to set up interviews, and that didn't go down well with the rest of the staff. So there were tensions between my day job and my comedy career.

However, while I was trying to balance the two and coming to the conclusion that one or the other would have to give, something totally unexpected took my mind off the problem. One day in 1990 Shelagh rang me at work and told me she was pregnant.

Chapter 8

Giant Steps

I was at once overjoyed and terrified. Shelagh and I had created a new life, but what would our child be like? Anyone who has been born with a disability lives with the shadow of fear that the deformity may be passed on to their children. Even though I'd been advised countless times that my phocomelia was a direct result of thalidomide damage and was not genetic, I couldn't help worrying.

Getting ready for the new arrival (I'm the one on the right, by the way).

Initially I was delighted, and relieved that I'd proved I could reproduce. That was something else that had always bothered me. Now at least I could be sure that I was normal in that respect – but would our baby be normal? It wasn't just thoughts and visions of deformities that haunted me but the knowledge that thalidomide had other less visible effects, such as malformations of the bowel and digestive system and damage to the ears. I had to do my best to put such fears out of my mind, and Shelagh and I planned for our baby like any other young married couple. My mum was over the moon, and during the pregnancy Shelagh and I were perhaps happier and more settled than we had been for a long time.

Even the early years of our marriage could be described as tempestuous at times, with neighbours complaining about our rows, and on odd occasions the police were called. At one point in 1988 Shelagh's dad had told us to split up if we couldn't get on better together and, to be honest, things hadn't improved much since then.

My lifestyle didn't help, because I was working by day and doing pubs and clubs at night. Shelagh had a part-time job at first in a local launderette, but I was happy for her to stay at home. I prided myself on being the breadwinner and I know that I always provided well for her, but perhaps I wasn't the best of company as I was often out or away. Of course we had good times too. But the bad times came often, and when they were bad they were horrid.

The prospect of the baby brought us closer together, and we were so happy when Hollie was born on 10 December 1990 at Liverpool's Mill Road Maternity Hospital. I was present at the birth, full of anxiety until the doctor showed me my newly washed daughter. He said,

'Here she is. Now will you believe she has five fingers and five toes on each hand and foot?'

I was so relieved, but my anxiety later proved to have a real basis as Hollie developed ear problems and eventually had to be fitted with grommets. It's a common enough condition in the general population but I can't help thinking that it could have been passed on to her from me as I myself suffer hearing problems, which I attribute to thalidomide damage.

Me with my daughter Hollie

By now I was quite a well-known figure in Liverpool and following Hollie's birth the *Liverpool Echo* published an article celebrating the event, in which I explained my fears and my relief at seeing our beautiful daughter.

These were busy years for me, working full time by day and performing at comedy venues most nights, so much of the care of our baby fell to Shelagh. I didn't see a problem with that then. I know attitudes have changed the last decade or so and modern men are now expected to take on their share of looking after babies but I was brought up in a traditional community where the men were expected to bring home the bacon and the women cooked it, so I suppose that was still in my mindset. Also I was conscious that I myself relied on Shelagh for help with personal care, and the amount of practical help I could give with Hollie was limited by my disability. It meant that I saw my role principally as that of provider, and I was determined to work as hard as I could for my wife and child and make sure they would never lack for anything.

There wasn't much time for leisure pursuits, but football has

Me with Shelagh and Hollie

always been my passion and my way of letting off steam. However, I had come to a point where I had to admit to myself that I was never going to be a star player and by 1992 I was concentrating on coaching and refereeing rather than active playing. But that year I was asked to take part in a penalty shoot-out sponsored by Carling, with celebrity guests. I wasn't a huge celebrity by any means, so I was pleased to be asked to participate.

It was a fun sort of event but, as in everything, my competitive spirit came to the fore. The first game was Oldham versus Ipswich and Miss World. This was back in the days when the Miss World competition was still running. I had to take a penalty against her, and I was told to lash the ball wide to let her win.

'What?' I said. 'No fucking chance.'

'No, Gary,' they said. 'She has to win.'

'Well get someone else to do it,' I said, but it was too late for that so I had to go on.

Out comes this dainty little thing in white shorts and white boots and stockings, and she's sort of poking the ball with her toes. I didn't give her any quarter but the goalie let all her balls in and did everything to keep mine out, so she won after all. I came off fuming. Like I've said earlier, I'm a terrible loser.

I didn't give any quarter as a ref, either. When I first took up refereeing I think my mates all thought I would favour them in the League games, but they couldn't have been more wrong. I'm a stickler for fair play, and besides that I really enjoyed the authority bestowed by blowing that whistle. It was very satisfying being obeyed after being at the beck and call of managers in my daytime job.

I was still working at Garston housing department but, although I'd been happy there at first, problems started to dog me again regarding my health and the need to take time off sick. Perhaps, because I had an alter ego as an up-and-coming comedian, people couldn't equate that with me having bouts of ill health and thought I was skiving off because of my supposedly hectic nightlife. As at Garston, it didn't go down well with some of my colleagues that I drove a big, expensive car and was frequently courted by the press, so that my name was often in the papers.

I was accused of all sorts of things, even fiddling tenancies for people, but none of it was true. I never did anything like that. It got so bad that I transferred from housing to the social services department and for a little while things were better, but mud sticks and soon it was being flung at me again.

The person who made allegations against me in the housing department lived next door to one of the workers in the social services department. They got talking one day and my name came up and the next thing the same stuff started up again, with this bloke giving me all kinds of grief. The worst thing about it was that I'd sort of befriended him, and I'd taken him along to a couple of my gigs. After that if I was ever off sick he'd say,

'Oh, you had a track record for this in the housing department.'

It actually did start to affect my health. I had a sort of breakdown and ended up on antidepressants. It wasn't me being over-sensitive. I was subjected to constant pressure that eventually took extreme forms, to the point where this man hired a private investigator to follow me about and took pictures of me in an effort to collect evidence that I was skiving when I was off sick. Incidentally, I found out recently that this same person no longer works for the council and has in fact become a down-and-out, so it just goes to show what goes around comes around. At the time, however, he was in a position of power, and he made my life a misery. I can only think it was all down to jealousy. When people came into the office they'd walk right past his desk and say,

'Oh, hello, Gary.' Everyone knew me, and they wanted to talk to me rather than him.

The job got so bad that I used to dread going in. After I had the breakdown I was retired on health grounds. The reason given was that I was unfit for duty because of my physical problems, managing toileting and my bouts of illness. I never like to give up on anything, but in a way it was a relief.

About this time I made a really good friend, George Devlin, who was to be a great help to me for many years. I met him when we were both support workers at Unicorn Street Day Centre, a facility for people with learning disabilities. We became very close, almost like brothers, and used to spend a lot of time together to the point that he neglected his own family to spend time with me. When Shelagh went into hospital to have our first child it was George who came to stay and look after me in her absence. However, I've always felt that this very closeness was at least partly responsible for the disaster that followed.

George's wife had always been a stay-at-home mum but she took a job as a school cleaner and she started having an affair with the school caretaker, who was a bit of a hard case from Norris Green. In those days I weighed thirteen and a half stone and I was pretty fit. I've always been able to look after myself despite my disability, and George was heartbroken about what was going on. So I went to the school where this caretaker worked. I could hear him whistling as he came down the corridor, and I was standing by the coal fire in his room. I just waited for him and he came in the door and saw me. He stopped whistling and said,

'What are you doing here? Who are you?'

I said, 'You don't know who I am, but you're about to find out. My mate's George Devlin and you're knocking his missis off. I'm telling you it's got to stop.'

He said, 'Who the fuck are you?'

I said, 'If I was you I'd find out who I am, and then I'd pack in.'

He said, 'I'm not fucking seeing anyone,'

I said, 'I know you are, and I'm telling you to pack it in.'

He said, 'Who the fucking hell do you think you are?'

I said, 'Listen, just do as you're fucking told or you're going to have to get out of town.'

Anyway Big Harold, one of the old Liverpool hard cases who used to run Croxteth Labour Club, phoned our house that night and he said,

'Now, now, Mr Skyner, calm down. Who have you been terrorising now?'

I asked why, and he said that this caretaker had rung him to find out who I was and he said to him,

'If Gary Skyner told you to get out of town you had better get out of town, because he knows everybody. What have you been doing to upset Gary?'

He said he would tip him the wink, but it ended up that George just couldn't cope with it. His wife was taking the morning-after pill in front of him and stuff like that, and he ended up giving her a belt. I got a phone call from Lower Lane police station to say he'd been arrested for it. I went down to the station to try and sort things out but George was drunk and singing like a canary in the interview room, when it would have been better if he'd kept quiet. Then when it came to explaining what had happened with his wife he shut up and never said a word. I wanted him to tell them how he'd been pushed to the limit, as she was blatantly carrying on in front of him… not that that excused him chinning her, but it might have gained him a little sympathy.

I did something to send a warning to this bloke and he got the hint. But instead of packing in he decided to have a go at George, daubing his car with paint and stuff, so it really got out of hand. George by then had left the matrimonial home and was living in Kirkby, but he kept going past the house and it was driving him mad. I gave him some advice about being rehoused and eventually he got a flat in Menlove Avenue among all the pensioners, and he was helping them with decorating and stuff. It took his mind off what had gone on, but gradually he hit the bottle.

George had always liked a drink, but after the divorce he went downhill big time. I would get phone calls from clubs and pubs all over town, even in the afternoons, asking me to come and collect him as he was causing trouble or was comatose somewhere. Those days comedy work was taking me further afield, and as he deteriorated the relationship became more difficult. Gradually I saw less and less of him but he was to come back in my life later, sadly under even worse circumstances.

I was doing really well in comedy. Signing with Steve Draper had opened up opportunities in other parts of the country as well as in my own region but, after following a tip from my former manager, Les Bather, I contacted an agent called Tony Jacobs, who was based in the north-east. I told him I was an established stand-up comedian in Merseyside looking for work further afield. His attitude was not encouraging, and in fact I thought he was an arrogant bastard. Our first conversation didn't go well and I put the phone down, neither expecting nor wanting to hear from him again.

I was surprised, then, when he contacted me a few days later to say he had been let down by another comic and wondered whether I could fill the slot. I was tempted to refuse till I heard the fee was £250. I did the gig. It went down well, and that was the start of a relationship that lasted for many years. Although Steve Draper remained my official manager I got lots of work from Tony, and became well known as a funny man on the north-east circuit.

By this time I was also starting to appear on television. In 1986 my first appearance was on BBC's *Kilroy* programme for Red Nose Day, alongside Ruby Wax and Leslie Crowther, to discuss taboos in comedy performance. In 1987, again for the BBC, I appeared in *The Marksman*, a *Play for Today* production about the Liverpool club scene. I had a bit part, and the main actor was Craig Charles. I was also featured on ITV News in 1987 after winning the title of Merseyside's King of Comedy. In 1989 I again took part in a discussion about taboos in comedy, this time for Channel 4's *Cutting Edge* programme. In this appearance I was invited to show how, as a disabled person, I justified telling jokes about disability. In 1992 I performed as one of the comedians in Granada TV's *The New Comedians*. There were other TV appearances during this time, but these were connected to the thalidomide campaign rather than to my comedy career.

Even though I was getting regular work as a comedian nothing is certain, and there is no guaranteed income in show business so I still felt I needed a day job to ensure security for my family. In my years with the council what I'd enjoyed most was working with disadvantaged people and trying to help them with their problems. In connection with work I'd done as a carer at the Unicorn Road Day Centre in Croxteth I had become a McKenzie friend (legal jargon for an unqualified advocate in court). I represented some of the people in my care who had mental health and learning difficulties.

One of the lawyers I got to know at this time suggested that my work was good enough for me to consider taking some legal training. I thought my experience would be useful in legal work while at the same time I would be able to gain a recognised qualification, so I wrote to a number of Liverpool legal firms. I was offered several positions without even having an interview and was taken on by Silverman Livermore, an old established firm of solicitors, as a trainee paralegal in May 1992.

The senior partner, Sir Harold Livermore, was one of the lead lawyers at the start of the Hillsborough case. He was due to retire, and I had the honour of being given his old office. I quickly established a large clientele and was fast becoming the 'king of the green forms.' The green form was the first form of legal aid, so that people who were on benefits could have legal work done up to the value of £92. Each matter would require a separate green form and, if you knew your stuff, each client would be eligible for at least four green forms.

My name soon became familiar in the local legal community as an up-and-coming paralegal and I was asked to open a welfare benefits department for Linskills Solicitors, who till then had largely dealt only with crime cases. This put me in a difficult situation, as I didn't want to upset my employers at Silverman Livermore. I spoke to my immediate boss and asked if it was OK for me to discuss the job with Linskills, but he told the senior partners. They obviously weren't happy, because the next thing I knew I was unceremoniously sacked. So my move to Linskills was assured, though not perhaps in the happiest of circumstances. My first week at Linskills coincided with a court appearance over my parking fines.

This was in May 1993, and I narrowly escaped being sent to prison. I'd had a number of parking tickets that I'd refused to pay because, to my mind, I should never have been given them in the first place. I had a disabled badge, which was always correctly displayed in my vehicle. Because of non-payment the fines had racked up to a tidy sum and, true to my stubborn nature, I still wouldn't pay.

The night before I was due in court I went out for a meal with a friend of mine, Eddie Ainsworth, and his girlfriend. They could see I wasn't my usual jokey self and asked what was up, so I told them the whole story. They laughed when I said I might be sent down the next morning.

'Oh, they won't send you to prison for that,' they said. I knew they could, theoretically, but thought it highly unlikely. However, there were around thirty-nine outstanding fines, and maybe they would want to make an example of me or punish me for being so stubborn.

Of course, when I arrived in court, all the local media were present: Radio City, Radio Merseyside and the *Liverpool Echo*. The charges, when they were read out, sounded pretty impressive. The original fines had escalated to a sum of nearly £1,500. The magistrates asked if I had anything to say so I went through my speech about how, as a disabled driver, I shouldn't have been ticketed in the first place. After conferring the chief magistrate, an elderly woman, began,

'Mr Skyner, we could jail you for a month,' and relief washed through me as I realised she wasn't going to put me away. Before she could finish the sentence, however, the prosecutor shot to his feet and intervened, saying,

'Madam, we insist on the maximum sentence. This has gone on far too long.'

There was another whispered conflab and then they sent me to prison for twenty-eight days. Even though I'd thought about the possibility I hadn't expected they would really do it, and I was in a daze as I was led down to the cells. I could hear the uproar in the court. People were shouting,

'That's not on, that.'

My mate Eddie, the one I'd been with the night before, was driving down the Dock Road when he heard the breaking news on Radio City that I'd been jailed. They must have got the news out almost instantaneously, as it was only ten minutes after the sentence had been passed down. Eddie was so surprised he nearly drove into the Mersey, and I found out later the switchboard at Canning Place was jammed with callers protesting that you couldn't do that to Gary.

I knew nothing of this though, as I was still down in the bridewell. An officer came to tell me I could make one phone call. Feeling angry and stubborn, I refused, saying,

'I don't need no phone call.' He grabbed me by the ear as if I was a soft schoolkid and said,

'Don't be fucking funny. You've got one phone call. Use it.'

Maybe they were frightened by all the media attention and were taking care to follow correct procedure. I don't know. Anyway, eventually I gave in and phoned Shelagh, but she just started giving me grief, saying,

'You're off your head, you. Why didn't you just pay up?' I was still sticking to my principles and I told her,

'I'm not paying fuck all.'

After that I was left to sit and reflect for what seemed a long time, but there was another lad down there and he said,

'Don't you work for a law firm?'

'Yes, I work for Linskills,' I said.

'Well, how come you're in here?' he said. I didn't feel like explaining to him so I just said,

'It's a long story.'

'Hey mate, you know me,' he said. 'Me girlfriend was carrying on with this fella,' and he started telling me how he hit him and did this and that, slashed the bloke's tyres and that was how he ended up next to me. 'They fucking put me in here. How bad's that?' He was really aggrieved.

I thought *Fucking hell. I'm locked up and I'm still getting asked for advice.* I wasn't in a sympathetic mood, so I turned round and said,

'Do me a favour and fuck off, will you?'

Next minute the door opened and a voice said, 'Gary Skyner? Come on, you can go.'

'No,' I said, 'I'm going nowhere.'

The copper said, 'You can go. Somebody's paid your fine. They've just sent a message down from upstairs.'

To this day I don't know who this anonymous do-gooder was. Actually I was a bit disappointed. I'd started to think of the opportunities for publicity that could arise from gaoling a thalidomide victim. I wasn't bothered about doing the time. They would have had to have kept me in the hospital wing, anyway. But it was funny. For days after I got home people were calling out in the street,

'How did you escape? You never climbed over the wall with your arms,' and stuff like that.

So I got let off, and it never even went on my record because I never actually left Cheapside. I was released at 12.20, just forty minutes before the prison van would have arrived to take me to Walton Prison. I don't know what happened. It still seems curious. I've heard rumours that the magistrates were told to quash the conviction because of the public outcry, but that must remain conjecture. Maybe the fines were just wiped out rather than paid by some benefactor, as a result of common sense prevailing after the event. We will never know.

I hadn't informed my superiors at Linskills of my impending court appearance, and following my release from the bridewell I just went back to work. However, the whole thing came out in the papers and the radio and, to my surprise, rather than being horrified my employer was pleased. He thought the publicity would make people realise I fought my corner and stood up for what I thought was right. He wasted no time in advertising the fact that I was head of his new welfare benefits section to the local media. The next thing I knew all my old clients from Silverman Livermore were on the phone booking appointments with me at Linskills.

I later moved to another firm called Ord & Co., who specialised in civil law, but it was while I was at Linskills that I began to develop an interest in reopening the thalidomide campaign. It was around this time that I first read the book *Suffer the Children*, which dealt with the first fight for compensation for the British thalidomide children (The *Sunday Times* Insight Team, 1979).

Until then I hadn't really known all the facts or fully understood the background of the development and marketing of the drug. Although my family had been part of it I hadn't taken too much notice of the struggle for compensation while I was growing up, but since my teens I'd developed a smouldering resentment towards the company that had made me the way I am. However, it was only after reading this book that the full horror and extent of the tragedy dawned on me.

I'd always thought that the development of thalidomide was some kind of mistake, something that the drug company couldn't really be blamed for. Now I realised how callousness and greed were at the root of the disaster, and that the condition of thousands of thalidomide children could so easily have been prevented.

I began to feel very angry but it was a formless sort of anger because I didn't know how to channel it into useful action, who to contact or what to do. It just kept playing on my mind that the thalidomide kids had been treated disgracefully, and that even though (with the help of The *Sunday Times*) a better settlement had been reached it was nowhere near enough.

My relationship with the Thalidomide Trust was deteriorating by this time, so I didn't want to seek advice there. It got up my nose that every time I wanted to buy something I had to go cap in hand and beg for the money, which I had to repay anyway from my annual allowance. In a normal compensation case you go to court and you are allocated a settlement, which you put in the bank. It's your money to do with as you please, but this isn't the case with the thalidomiders.

What makes it worse is that we only got a fraction of what we should have received in the first place. I can't help thinking that when DCBL first agreed the settlement they thought (should I say 'hoped') that we wouldn't live all that long, but most of us survived into the 1990s. By then we were all in our thirties, and many of us had families to support. Our expenses were growing with our adult care needs, while at the same time inflation had eaten away at the value of the Trust Fund.

It hadn't been too bad when Group Captain Gardener had been in charge of distributing the money (until 1983). Under his administration most applications were authorised without too much difficulty, but once Neil Buckland took over it got worse and worse. He was like the man from Del Monte, but who always said 'No'.

Buckland was an accountant, and his sole motivation seemed to be to save the Trust's money. I suppose the rationale for this was to keep back money for investment so that the fund would grow, but he seemed to lose sight of the fact that the Trust was there for the benefit of us thalidomiders in the first place. Every time I needed something it became a battle, and after several years of this I'd had enough. It wasn't just the parsimonious attitude and the feeling of having to beg for what you were entitled to that I objected to. The assessment procedures used by the Trust seemed similarly designed to make you feel like an unworthy beggar.

The annual allowance is calculated on the degree of disability. Basically you get so much for the lack of an arm, the lack of a leg, the lack of two arms, the lack of two legs...

and so on. That is, if you are 'lucky' enough to qualify in the first place. Many applicants have been dismissed through lack of evidence of the drug being taken during pregnancy or because their condition did not reflect the classic symptoms of thalidomide damage. Some of these may have been genuine claimants (over the years the ramifications of thalidomide damage have proved to be hard to identify precisely).

Having passed the initial 'test', and having been accepted as thalidomide damaged, any further reassessment depends on my requesting a review. This involves being interviewed by a dedicated member of the Trust staff in the presence of another thalidomider as chaperone, to ensure that things are done correctly. I suppose the function of this review is to benefit us, in the sense that it should pick up any increased care needs.

In those years I couldn't help feeling that the Trust had always leant towards minimising the financial liability incurred by DCBL, then Guinness and now Diageo, the current owners of the company that supplied thalidomide in Britain. But that was my personal opinion, and I don't think my attitude was shared by most other thalidomide victims. Thankfully, I think the Trust has moved on in later years and is becoming more proactive on our behalf.

I was brought up in normal society and have fought all my life to be treated as normal in that society. I expect to have the same man-to-man relationship in my dealings with the Trust. Many thalidomide victims have never had the independence that I expect as a right. They were brought up in institutions or went to residential schools or special schools where they have been accustomed to life in a paternalistic social bubble, sheltered from making their own decisions and standing up for themselves.

My situation has two effects. It makes me appear a wild card to the Trust, because I don't agree with everything they say and I'm not afraid to protest and say what I think. It also makes me a wild card with fellow thalidomiders, because dependency is anathema to me. Most thalidomiders see themselves as a cohesive minority group sharing similar lives, and the Trust for them is a kind of protective umbrella to which they can turn for help and advice. I've always resisted this kind of inclusion. I don't consider myself disabled, and I've always made every effort to be as normal as possible.

By 1992 I was becoming increasingly resentful towards Guinness/DCBL and the Thalidomide Trust, but what finally pushed me to take action was a run-in with the Trust over my car. I'd bought a new Nissan Primera with authorisation from the Trust. I needed a good, reliable car for work, as I was now travelling all over the country. After a year I accidentally broke the car aerial. I could just have got it fixed, but when I went to the dealership I decided to upgrade to a bigger three-litre model and paid the difference out of my own pocket.

Unfortunately a year later I was involved in an accident that caused £2,000 of damage to the car, so I contacted the Trust to make a claim on the insurance. I was amazed at Neil Buckland's reaction. He told me off as if I was a naughty child for getting the bigger car without his permission and even implied that, as a thalidomider, I was not capable of driving such a powerful vehicle. The tirade ended with him refusing to allow me to claim through the insurance, which meant that I had to find the money myself.

This is the kind of paternalistic treatment that really rubs me up the wrong way, and while other thalidomiders might take it lying down I wasn't going to. I wrote to my MP (at the time this was Eddie Loyden) asking why I had to go begging to the Trust for money, and why the government and the company responsible for selling thalidomide in this country had not paid proper compensation to us thalidomiders.

Three months went by while I waited for a response,

but then one morning in early 1993 I heard on Radio City's breakfast news that a Liverpool thalidomide victim was seeking to reopen the compensation case. I'd been having a lie-in, but suddenly I was fully awake. I leapt out of bed and turned the radio up. Naturally I thought they were talking about me, and that Eddie Loyden had issued a press release without consulting me. I thought that a bit strange, but I was elated that the proposed case was getting publicity. However, the newsreader went on to say,

'Freddie Astbury, a thalidomide victim from Croxteth Park, has launched an appeal via the European courts to reopen the thalidomide case.'

Freddie Astbury, looking ready to do battle.

I knew many of the presenters on Radio City and I immediately contacted Graham White, who put me in touch with Freddie. Despite our shortages of arms and legs two heads are definitely better than one, and the fact that there were now at least two of us gave us strength to support each other and to create a viable attack on Guinness.

Freddie had contacted the Liverpool MEP Ken Stewart, who had voiced a willingness to help. His involvement lent authority to our campaign, and helped to create serious media interest.

Guinness agreed to meet us to discuss our concerns, but before this meeting could take place we were invited to appear on Granada TV's programme *This Morning*, with Richard and Judy. The interview took place at the Granada studios in the Albert Dock, and we got a very sympathetic reception. Jacqueline Perry, who was the in-house lawyer for Granada, was there to ensure that nothing said in the programme might result in a lawsuit. She was a lovely girl, and she asked us to keep in touch and to let her know if she could do anything to help. The interview itself was a great opportunity for us to make the British public aware of our plight and to show that we were determined to fight for justice and a fair deal, not just for ourselves but for all the British thalidomiders.

It was lucky for me that I'd chosen to work in the field of law. Although Linskills (my employer at the time) specialised mainly in criminal law, Roy Whitelaw (a trainee with the company) was gaining expertise in personal injury. With his help and advice we applied for legal aid in December 1994 in order to try to reopen the compensation case.

When we heard nothing from the Legal Aid Agency, despite repeated phone calls, Freddie decided to up the ante by going on hunger strike on 18 December. The news spread quickly through the media. It made a good story, especially just before Christmas and the season of goodwill. Guinness, no doubt with one eye to possible adverse publicity and boycotting of their products during what was probably their best sales period of the year, immediately proposed a meeting with Freddie. Now, we thought, we were getting somewhere. Freddie agreed to the meeting, but stipulated that Roy Whitelaw and I should also be present.

The meeting took place on 20 December at Freddie's home. Maybe we felt better on our home turf but this proved to be a misjudgement on our part, as the two Guinness representatives were much taken with Freddie's possessions – most notably with his huge TV and expensive sound system. It maddened me to see their attitude. They were obviously thinking that if we could afford such luxuries we shouldn't be crying poverty to them. They didn't spare a thought for the fact that such items were Freddie's only distractions from a life mainly spent restricted to his home.

To our disappointment it was clear from the start that they weren't bringing any sensible discussion of our needs to the table, but had only come to offer a sop to shut us up. They had allowed only a 45-minute time slot for the meeting, and shot off in a pre-booked taxi once they'd delivered their humiliating proposals. Again we were to be treated as charity cases. Their offer was to see what they could spare from charitable donations allocated for the year and to whisper in parliamentary ears to try to get some tax concessions for the Trust – all delivered with phoney smiles and fake concern, which left me fuming.

There is always something to be learnt from every experience, good or bad, and what we took away from this one was to set any future meetings on neutral ground in order to focus on the business in hand, and not on our surroundings and lifestyles.

Freddie remained on hunger strike and, in view of the condition of his general health, he soon began to deteriorate. On 23 December Sue Astbury phoned to say that Freddie had been taken into hospital and, on Christmas Eve morning, I opened my *Daily Post* to see this headline:

Thalidomide Hunger Striker Lapses Into Coma.

Roy Whitelaw and I hurried down to the legal aid office and refused to leave until we got a decision, even if it meant spending Christmas there. Although the case worker made us wait two hours the news headlines obviously did the trick. At 12.30 pm we walked out with a legal aid certificate authorising us to seek a junior barrister's opinion on the merits of reopening the case. It meant the end of Freddie's hunger strike, and he soon recovered his health and was sent home from hospital.

Christmas is a magic time for kids, and it was wonderful seeing Hollie's face light up at the decorations and her delight in opening her presents. We had all the usual fun and festivities, but for me getting that legal aid certificate was the best gift I could have asked for.

Chapter 9

Pissing in the Wind

At the same time as our campaign in the UK was gaining strength, thalidomide again hit the news in the USA. There is a common saying that nothing is ever entirely bad, and another that every cloud has a silver lining. So it proved with thalidomide. The drug that produces horrifying birth defects was found to be efficacious in treating the symptoms of one of the world's most dreaded endemic diseases… leprosy.

How was this discovered, since the production and distribution of the drug was halted once its teratogenic properties were confirmed? In 1964 Dr Jacob Sheskin, a specialist in the treatment of leprosy who was then working in Jerusalem, was sent a patient suffering from a severe and terribly painful complication of the disease. This condition is known as erythema nodosum leprosum (ENL), in which the patient suffers large boils over the whole body. In severe cases the patient, prevented by the pain from sleeping or eating properly, rapidly wastes away to the point of death.

Nothing seemed to alleviate the condition to allow Sheskin's patient to improve. In desperation Sheskin searched through the hospital pharmacy while looking for something that might give his patient respite to get some sleep… and there he came upon a forgotten bottle of thalidomide tablets.

(Although this proved to be a godsend it just shows how, although withdrawn, thalidomide tablets could linger on in the back of medicine cabinets for years like ticking time bombs). Sheskin remembered that thalidomide had in the past been prescribed as a sleeping tablet and, as his patient was close to death anyway, he felt there was nothing to lose in trying it.

The resulting improvement was dramatic. The boils disappeared over a very short period and the patient made a rapid recovery. The same result was replicated when the drug was trialled on other patients.

Dr Sheskin moved to Venezuela, where thalidomide was still legally available, and after conducting clinical trials he published the amazing results in 1965. The research was then taken up on a larger scale by the World Health Organisation, and it was found that 99% of sufferers showed total remission of symptoms after just two weeks of treatment.

Although thalidomide remained banned in Europe and the USA it continued to be available in South America, where leprosy is still a serious problem. However, supplies were difficult to obtain. The only source was the original makers, Chemie Grünenthal, who still held the patent. Some supplies had been stockpiled at Grünenthal's headquarters since the drug was withdrawn from sale in most countries at a high point of its popularity (and, hence, production). (Brynner and Stephens (2001) point out the ironic fact that Dr Sheskin, a European Jew who had been forced to hide in a Polish ghetto during World War II, had to negotiate with the former Nazi Heinrich Mückter and even to collaborate with him on research papers about the drug.)

After this companies in Venezuela began producing the drug themselves, often not to rigorous standards. Babies with classic thalidomide-induced birth defects began to appear once again, even though precautions were taken to warn against the deadly teratogenic effects of thalidomide. This didn't come to official attention until decades later, despite the fact that the drug had been in use since the late 1960s. Official research conducted in 1996 identified thirty-four defective births. But, as always, the real figure is probably much higher, if we consider unreported defects and infants who died *in utero.*

By the 1980s AIDS was becoming the world's new horror disease. As it is an inflammatory disease that attacks the immune system, as leprosy does, questions were raised as to whether thalidomide might be useful in treating symptoms of the disease.

Although the value of thalidomide in treating leprosy was proven at this point the exact way in which the drug worked remained unknown. However, the work of Dr Gilla Kaplan in the 1980s revealed the action of thalidomide on the human immune system. She worked out that the drug enabled the compromised immune system to right itself in order to fight inflammation.

In 1993 Kaplan showed that thalidomide was effective in suppressing the latent form of HIV Type 1 but, to proceed further, a safe supply of the drug was essential. Although thalidomide was readily available on the black market, and was probably already being widely self-administered by people who were HIV-positive, this was far from a satisfactory situation. Not only was the quality of the drug being supplied in question, but self-administration also created the possibilities of inappropriate use... and the potential for the deadly side effects of the drug to surface once more.

In 1994 the US Food and Drug Administration (the FDA or the USFDA), whose former director Frances Kelsey had been decorated for refusing to license thalidomide in the 1960s, agreed to consider an application to approve the use of thalidomide in the US for the treatment of AIDS.

Meanwhile, back in the UK, in January 1994 we secured

a legal aid certificate for £30,000 to pay for a senior barrister's opinion on the merits of reopening the case against DCBL/ Guinness. This was in Freddie Astbury's name.

After that everybody turned up at the Thalidomide Society's meeting. You couldn't get a room in the Crest Hotel in Runcorn. At least forty people turned up because they all wanted to know what Freddie and I were doing, and everyone was hoping that this was a breakthrough. Freddie's not the best public speaker, so I got up. I told everyone that what we were doing was trying to reopen the case on the grounds that the parents had been unduly coerced into signing the original agreement without being able to make an informed judgment, and I told them that we had a legal aid certificate.

The week before a solicitor, Chris Lingard, who is a thalidomider with shorter arms than me, rang me and said,

'Quite frankly, I think you're pissing in the wind.'

I said, 'Well, I don't.'

During the night after the meeting he said to Freddie that he was part of a big London firm, and that it would be better for them to take over the case. Jacqueline Perry, the Granada TV solicitor we'd met when we appeared on *This Morning* with Richard and Judy, had kept in touch with us. She advocated getting a London brief, and suggested Anthony Scrivener. Freddie went along with Chris Lingard, and moved his case down to London. I was angry about this, but there was nothing I could do. I approached Kevin Donellan, who has similar thalidomide damage to Freddie, and I said,

'If we got a certificate for Freddie we can get one for you,' so then we had two certificates running at the same time exploring the same case.

For our choice of barrister Roy Whitelaw and I favoured George Carman. Julian Linskill, my employer, recommended Timothy King. Linskills wasn't really the best firm to deal with the case but we ended up choosing Timothy King, who had been involved in the Hillsborough case. He was chosen partly because his offices were in Manchester, so he was easily accessible for us. But when we received his opinion it was unfavourable regarding our chances, so we had to look elsewhere. A second opinion from Anthony Scrivener was not much better. Both barristers agreed that the agreements signed by our parents in 1973 were still binding, and therefore the case was now statute barred and couldn't be reversed. It seemed that we had come to a dead end.

During this period Guinness, which had bought up DCBL, merged with another smaller company named Grand Metropolitan. They renamed the resultant new firm Diageo. We felt that one way forward was to lobby the company, so Freddie and I bought shares in order to be able to attend shareholders' meetings and hopefully be able to influence the other shareholders.

Eventually Diageo decided to pay a top-up to the Thalidomide Trust Fund. It was a far cry from what we wanted, but it was a start. I think it was only our actions that achieved this result. The threat of hunger strikes and resulting media publicity, plus the backup of the legal aid certificate and the possibility of lengthy court action, probably moved them this way.

They probably thought that chucking us a few crumbs would satisfy us, but they didn't know my reputation for stubbornness and determination. When Mr Davidson, the Guinness representative dealing with the matter, called me to tell me they'd decided to pay the £2.5 million, I said,

'Fine. That'll do for me. Now... what about the other thalidomiders?'

You don't have to be a maths genius to work out that £2.5 million shared between 455 disabled people amounts to little more than an insult, especially when you consider that the firm's profits stood at billions of dollars a year at the end of the twentieth century.

What made it worse was this. After the money was finally paid the Trust announced that, while it would help to maintain the Trust's financial viability for the future, it wouldn't provide any increase in payments to us, the beneficiaries – or at least it would not provide an increase of more than 0.5%.

Around this time I had another run-in with the Trust over an extension to my house that I wanted to build. I expected problems with Neil Buckland, and I wasn't disappointed. He agreed to allow the extension providing it was a large single-storey building rather than the two-storey structure I'd planned. This was a crafty move, as he knew the structure would spoil the appearance of the house and that the neighbours would object to planning permission. I thought, *Well, I can box clever too, if that's how you want to play it.*

Shelagh wanted the extension, and I was determined that she should get what she wanted. I had two sets of plans made: one for the extension Buckland suggested, and one for the one we wanted. Buckland agreed the finances, and I got on with building my extension and congratulated myself on outwitting him. I'd underestimated him, though, because the next thing he did was to hire a private investigator to come and take photos of the developing structure, from which it was plain it was no single-storey building. He obtained copies from the local planning office of the plans that had actually been passed, and then wrote to me to say that the rest of the money for the extension would not be paid from Trust funds.

It was a nightmare that I unsuccessfully tried to argue my way out of, saying that Buckland's intractability had caused me to go to such lengths of deception. The builder was threatening to sue me if I didn't pay up, and I didn't know what to do. In desperation I wrote a strong letter to the board of the Trust. I knew that Lord Justice Griffiths presided as chairman, and he would have the final word. After a short period of nail-biting Griffiths handed down his verdict to Buckland. Although I was castigated for my dishonesty the rest of the money was paid by the Trust, to avoid my being sued by the builder.

I got off the hook but it was yet another black mark on my card, and a serious one at that. However, it brought home to me how inadequate the new settlement from Diageo really was, and made me even more determined to pursue it further. It wasn't good enough, and I and the few thalidomiders who were brave enough to stand up and fight began to plan a further campaign. This time we expected more difficulty because Diageo probably thought it had done enough for us, with the top-up being so recent, so we expected to have a fight on our hands. We didn't have much faith in the company where fair dealing was concerned.

In 1990 (when the company was still known as Guinness) the chairman Ernest Saunders, together with other executives, was convicted of insider dealing and given a five-year prison sentence. Saunders, however, was released in August 1991 following claims that he was suffering from progressive Alzheimer's disease. We didn't have much faith in the management of the company, and the measly nature of the current top-up showed the extent of their commitment to us.

The experience of the original campaign against DCBL in the 1970s had shown that only when the company was threatened with boycott of their products and massive loss of income were they moved to pay serious attention to compensating the victims of the drug they had made so much profit from. When Guinness had taken over DCBL, under Saunders' leadership, the company had the audacity to argue that the past was nothing to do with it. It was happy to take on Distillers' assets, but not so keen on accepting its liabilities.

Our solicitors for this offensive were the London firm of Leigh Day & Co. One angle we were keen to pursue was the possibility that thalidomide might cause genetic damage, which could be passed on to future generations. With this in mind we obtained a legal aid certificate for Glen and Debbie Harrison. Glen had been accepted as a 'late' thalidomide victim because of damage to one hand. His eligibility had originally been questioned due to the fact that his deformity didn't correspond exactly with the classic symptoms of thalidomide damage, and it was only with time that it was realised that thalidomide symptoms can be very varied. However, his own children had been born with similar deformities to his own, and this bolstered our argument that thalidomide could pass on its terrible effects through the DNA of its victims.

This idea had been proposed and argued by William McBride, the Australian paediatrician who had first uncovered the thalidomide tragedy, and accordingly we invited him to come to England in 1996 to discuss the merits of our case.

McBride is certainly a major figure in the thalidomide story. Thanks to his making the connection between the rash of birth defects that appeared in the early 1960s and the drug, thousands of babies were saved from death or deformity in Australia and, once his warnings were heeded, across the rest of the world. In 1971 McBride received a gold medal from *l'Institut de la Vie* in Paris and was able to set up his own research facility in Australia. Sadly, he was later dogged by scandal and he was largely discredited in medical and academic circles due to a much publicised case involving a drug called Bendectin, which was prescribed for morning sickness in the same way that thalidomide had been used and produced by the American firm Merrell Dow, (formerly Richardson-Merrell). Based on evidence provided by McBride regarding the drug's properties many lawsuits were brought against the company by parents whose children had been born with defects after using Bendectin. However, McBride's claims – supposedly based on the results of clinical tests – were later denied in court by his own laboratory workers. As a result he was vilified and his licence to practise medicine was actually revoked in 1993, but reinstated in 1998 (Brynner and Stephens, 2001).

I found McBride a larger-than-life character. His Irish ancestry showed in a fondness for drink, and he demonstrated a short fuse sometimes when he'd had a few. I recall us almost being thrown out of an Indian restaurant in Stanley Street in Liverpool, where we had gone for a meal. He treated me to a long explanation of how thalidomide caused genetic damage. It was full of chemical formulae and medical jargon and I didn't understand it, and I said,

'It's all double Dutch to me, Bill.' He must have thought I doubted him – and maybe his recent difficulties in academic circles still rankled, because he got quite argumentative and colourful (to the surprise of other diners) and eventually banged on the table to emphasise his point. He accompanied me and Elizabeth Ord, my then employer, to see Glen and Debbie Harrison, and he remained adamant that thalidomide could alter DNA in the womb and thus pass defects on to the children of thalidomide victims.

All this campaigning plus having two jobs – legal work by day and comedy at night – was taking a toll on my personal life and putting a strain on our marriage, which had always had its ups and downs. My weight was steadily increasing, as my lifestyle wasn't geared to healthy eating. I've always been a bit of a big lad, but I was never severely overweight when young.

Around 1985 I did my cruciate ligaments in and I had treatment for them, but I was never the same afterwards. That's when I started piling on the pounds, and I just kept buying bigger clothes. It got to the stage in 1987 when we were staying in a hotel up in the Lakes, and my heart was racing. I didn't tell Shelagh how bad it was but I thought, *I'd better sort this out or it'll sort me out.*

I wasn't as big as I have been recently but then I went on

a weight loss programme and started taking Duromine and staying off the ale, and I got down to 12 stone something again. I was doing a lot of running round Sefton Park around the time when Hollie was born. You can see on the photos that I was really fit but then I started comfort eating again, and then I made friends with Eddie and Stacey and we were always going out for meals and stuff. I do a lot of sportsmen's dinners, cabarets and so on, so the lifestyle didn't help. But basically I was just eating, because it didn't seem to matter how big I got.

I wasn't the happiest of people during these years, despite my outward happy-go-lucky front. Perhaps this was partly responsible for my not taking care of my health properly, and it could also have been the reason why I sometimes fell by the wayside when temptation reared its head.

Some years earlier I'd been doing a gig at a club whose bill also featured a male stripper who performed with a python. While I was setting up my gear on stage before the show a very attractive woman came up to me and said she thought we were related. We chatted and it turned out that her uncle was married to my cousin, so although we were related there was no blood tie. She was a lovely-looking girl – I'll call her Sylvia – but I didn't think anything more of it. As a comic I was used to girls chatting me up despite my disability and I'd learnt how to flirt back, but that's as far as it usually went.

Anyway, this stripper came on and went into his routine. He had the snake in a bag, which he asked me to hold for him. He didn't tell me what was in it, and I nearly threw a wobbler when I saw the bag start to move. At first he was just doing a straight strip and all the women were egging him on, with Sylvia at the forefront. He got his kit off, hiding the essentials behind a towel, and then he picked Sylvia out of the audience and blindfolded her. The next thing he did was pull the python out of the bag and everybody screamed, but Sylvia must have thought he was showing them his penis. He put the python's head up to her face and told her to open her mouth but she opened her eyes, saw the snake right in front of her and promptly fainted. They had to call an ambulance and give her oxygen, but after that she recovered and the rest of the evening went off OK.

A few years later I went on a visit with a colleague to a house in West Derby Road to see an elderly client who was becoming confused. When we knocked on the door who should open it but Sylvia? I remembered her instantly. Well, who could forget those circumstances? It turned out that she was our client's carer so we got talking, and she asked to come to one of my gigs.

When we got back in our car, my colleague said,

'I think you've clicked there.'

I said, 'Fuck off. She wouldn't pick me up with two shitty sticks.'

When I got to work the next day there were six phone messages from her asking me to call. So I did, and asked what the emergency was, thinking it was something to do with our client. She'd actually made some excuse that she had a query about the client, but then she got to asking how I was and what I was doing and so on.

This kept happening. It got to the stage where she was ringing up every couple of hours, so in the end I stopped returning her calls. She was taking up so much of my working day that I had to stay late every night to get my paperwork done. Shortly after this I was called into the boss's office one evening and he said,

'Why are you neglecting my clients?'

I said, 'You what?'

He said, 'I've had a very irate lady on the phone, and she wants to know why you're not returning her calls.'

I said, 'She's gaga. That's why. You come to my office and see how many calls I've already put through to her.'

'Well, she's not happy,' he said, 'and I like my clients to be happy. You must return her calls.'

I said,'What can I tell her? I can't say any more than I already have.'

He said, 'Well, I want you to ring her as a matter of courtesy.'

Shortly after this I left Linskills and went to work for another law firm, but on my birthday a big cake in the shape of a whisky bottle turned up at the office. All the girls were taking the piss out of me, saying,

'Who's it off, then?' and stuff. I had a good idea and I wasn't too happy about it.

The next thing I saw this bloke coming down Water Street. My office was in the basement so I could see up to street level and could see people's legs passing by. These trouser legs were very close, so I looked up and saw the bloke was carrying a big bunch of balloons with *Happy Birthday* and *Lots of Love* written on them. One of the girls said,

'I bet they're for you, Gaz.'

I said, 'Oh, fuck off. Don't be daft,' but then the next minute he walked in with them and said, 'Gary Skyner?'

A bit later on a bottle of champagne was delivered too. I was in a daze but I found out later that Sylvia had once gone out with a fireman and she'd done the same to him, sending presents and messages all the time.

At first I was flattered, but I had no intention of starting an affair. My colleagues at work all thought I was knocking her off but I wasn't. I knew if we did start something it wouldn't just be a casual affair. I really was attracted to her but she went over the top. She just wouldn't leave me alone, and in the end I did cave in and we had an affair. As I'd expected it quickly got more serious than I wanted it to. I had no intention of leaving my wife and child, but she was intent on persuading me to do just that.

I began trying to extricate myself. Not only was I terrified of getting caught and Shelagh finding out, but she was interfering with my work and also making me a target of fun with my colleagues. That was bad enough, but alarm bells really started ringing when she started driving from her home in Formby to sit outside my house in her car. I kept telling her I was a married man, but despite all my misgivings I took her to Barrow with me one night for a show. When we were driving she said to me,

'I want you to leave home.'

I said, 'What? Are you fucking mad?'

She said, 'No,' but I just started laughing. I thought she was winding me up, that my mates had put her up to it. She said,

'If there wasn't a child involved I know you would leave.' Then she started hitting me, really punching me and crying. She kept saying, 'Leave home... I love you.'

I ended up black and blue. The next day Shelagh was giving me a shower and she asked me where all the bruises had come from, and I had to say I'd fallen off the stage at the gig. She must have thought I'd had a scrap with someone. You wouldn't have thought a woman could have done it.

But, even after all that, I couldn't just break it off. She was a beautiful woman, very glamorous, sort of a cross between Jill Dando and Princess Diana. My colleagues used to say,

'What's she doing with you?' and I'd say,

'Fucked if I know.'

They'd say, 'Well, you must be well hung.'

I used to reply, 'Well, she wouldn't know if I am,' because at that time nothing was going on between us. There was something there, though, besides just sex. If I ever thought about leaving home it would have been for her. However, I couldn't go. Shelagh and Hollie depended on me.

It came to a head when Sylvia gave me an ultimatum.

'If you don't leave home by 6 November you'll never see me again.'

I don't know why she chose that date, which was the day after my birthday. So 6 November came and she phoned the office and asked the secretary if I was in and the secretary said that I was, and Sylvia asked,

'Has he got any clothes in the back of his car?' and the secretary didn't know, so Sylvia asked to speak to me. I was with a client so she rang off. I had a full client list that day and I told the secretary at lunchtime not to put her through if she rang. At four o'clock she turned up outside and she said,

'You haven't left her, have you?' and I told her that I couldn't. She started calling me all kinds of bastards.

That evening I had to go to Leicester to a comedy job. When you're on stage being the funny man people don't realise what kind of heartbreak and problems you can be hiding. That's what being professional is all about. All night I was thinking, *She's going to blow me up now*, and as I was driving back my mobile rang and it was Sylvia's mother. She started to lay into me, saying,

'I just want to tell you… You are an absolute bastard. You know how to press all the buttons, buying my daughter cuddly toys, taking her out and buying her flowers…' I felt bad, but I said,

'It's nothing to do with you. Where is she now?'

She said, 'Like the stupid girl she is she's sitting in your road.'

I nearly crashed the car. I just went numb and I thought, *It's all over. My marriage is over. Everything's fucked.* Anyway I came round the corner and my headlights picked out her number plate just up the road from my house. I made her get in my car and drove to a field at the back of the houses and she pleaded and pleaded with me to leave and I said,

'I just can't do it. I've got a kid.'

She said, 'You'll never ever see me again,' and, true to her word, I never have.

I've had a couple of blips. Later I heard she was a paramedic working out of Southport hospital and once or twice I've driven to Southport and driven round the hospital car park, hoping I might see her. So there was clearly something there on my part. I've given paramedics my card and asked them to tell her to ring me. It wasn't that I wanted to rekindle anything. I just wanted her to understand where I was coming from and I hoped maybe we could still be mates, that's all. I suppose I've been a bad lad.

Did Shelagh know? I've never been sure, but I suspect she did. I always think women know when something is going on. It was about that time when she wanted to try for another baby, and I agreed. For me it was a sort of way of putting myself straight, sort of telling myself, *Well, you're a married man. You should live up to it.* It was a way of reassuring Shelagh and of making a statement that I wanted to repair things and make a go of it, even though by then I felt there was little love between us and we were drifting apart. Otherwise I wouldn't have so easily got involved with someone else.

Shelagh became pregnant in 1996, and we settled down to await the new arrival. However, a shock was in store for me later that year. I was still then working at Ord's legal firm, and one day Shelagh phoned me to say that something had happened and I had to come home right away. Of course I panicked and rushed off, thinking of all sorts of disasters that might have befallen as I drove home.

But what I found there was the last thing I would have expected.

Gary's Hall of Fame

A tribute to the just a few of the many personalities I have been fortunate to meet and work with in my career.

Ricky Tomlinson, who has been a great friend and support to me in my career and in the thalidomide campaigns. Pictured here with Barry Fry at Peterborough United, May 2013.

Kevin Donellan, a stalwart thalidomide campaigner. Pictured here with Ricky and me during the Government Health Grant campaign 2009.

MY ARSE!

FRIDAY 20TH MAY, 2011   £35   STABLES, BOLHOLT HOTEL

AN EVENING WITH RICKY TOMLINSON

PLUS COMEDIAN GARY SKYNER, AUCTION AND CHARITY RAFFLE

ERIC TOMLINSON (born 26 September 1939), known by his stage name Ricky Tomlinson, is an English actor and comedian, best known for his roles as DCI Charlie Wise in Cracker and James "Jim" Royle in The Royle Family.

Tomlinson was born Eric Tomlinson in Bispham, Blackpool, Lancashire, but has lived in Liverpool for most of his life. Tomlinson was born in Bispham because his mother, Peggy, was evacuated there due to the Liverpool Blitz in World War II. In 1962 he married his first wife Marlene, and they went on to have three children.

Turn to Page 2

Sammy McIlroy and Alan Hudson with me in 1992.

With Sir Harold Evans, former editor of The Sunday Times on publication of his book, My Paperchase: True Stories of Vanished Times, in 2009

With Keith Senior from Leeds Rhinos in York, 2013.

Getting chinned by Nigel Benn, while Smithy, John Smith Snr, just laughs. Castleford, 2014.

A motley crew assembled for The Match pilot comedy show for ITV 2014. Including Michael Starke, Brendan Healy, Paul Boardman, Mick Miller, Stan Boardman, Ron Atkinson… and, of course, yours truly.

With Jan Molby at Hundith Hill Hotel, Cumbria, May 2015.

With Evander Holyfield. He's not really going to thump me (I hope).
Castleford, West Yorkshire 2014.

Pat Van Den Hauwe and Andy Nicholls, author of Scally.
Alan Stubbs's wine bar, Birkdale, 2012.

The Laughter Factory for the James Bulger Memorial Trust. Chung Ku,
Riverside Drive, Liverpool

Chapter 10

That's Showbiz

I walked in the door to find my dad and Marge sitting on our sofa. I got the shock of my life and said the first thing that came into my head.

'To what do I owe the pleasure?'

It was an awkward situation. I didn't feel any emotion for him or joy at seeing him. We made small talk for a while and he told us they had come over to visit Marge's family, and he had been to see his brother and sister. I thought he had only come to see me because he knew I would find out that he had been visiting my aunt and uncle and it would have looked bad for him not to contact Karen and me.

I thought it would be a good idea to go out together with Karen for a family meal. At least it would be on neutral ground, so we made a date to meet the following Tuesday afternoon for lunch at the Britannia on Otterspool Prom. I rang Karen and arranged it, but I didn't tell my mum. I could hardly ask her along if Marge was going to be sitting there, as even after all these years my mum still carried a lot of bitterness about what had happened. So did I, for that matter.

It was a strange meal. I was polite towards my dad, but that was all. Really, I didn't feel any emotion at seeing him. They were staying at the St George Hotel and I said they could have easily stayed with us, at which point Marge jumped in and said,

'We don't put on people, and we don't like to be put upon.' I took this as a message that if ever I went to Australia I was not to expect them to put me up. I just kept my cool and ignored her bad manners, and let Karen do all the talking.

Karen had told my mum that she hated our dad, but that day she was all over him like a rash. I just sat there without saying much, to show my distaste for what he'd done to my mum, but Karen was acting like Daddy's girl all over again. It didn't get her anywhere, because after he got home he just blanked her like he did me. He never sent her or her kids a birthday card or anything.

My car was in for repair, so when it came time to go home I phoned for a taxi. As I was getting in it my dad got hold of my arm. I saw he was crying, but it didn't make me feel anything for him. I said,

'This is probably the last time you'll see me.'

He said, 'Yeah,' and I shut the taxi door and I was gone. I had no emotion, except that I remembered how he'd acted at my Granddad Skyner's funeral and how I'd nearly killed him then.

I wondered why he was crying, and I could only think it was guilt. He knew what he'd done and how he'd acted towards me all my life, carrying on as if I would never be capable of anything. Now, on coming back to England, he would have heard about how I'd overcome my problems to become a successful comedian and how I had married and raised a family like any normal person. He'd written me off and left me, and I'd proved him wrong. He'd put me down as a no-hoper from the start, so maybe it was easier for him to go off to Australia with Marge. It must have made him feel bad to find he was a million miles off the track.

I waited till he'd gone back to Australia before I told my

mum about the meeting. I had to tell her because she would soon have found out from relatives, but I knew there would be trouble and I wasn't wrong. I got loads of stick from her when all I'd done was sit there, eat my meal and pick up the bill. I'd barely spoken to him or Marge. My mum was furious. She said,

'Oh, you organised it, you paid for it and you never told me or thought to ask me.'

I said, 'How could I ask you? How could you go there with the other one sitting there? There would have been murder, and you know it.'

Mum said, 'After all I've done for you and stuck by you, and you think the world of him,' etc., etc. I tried to tell her I'd really had nothing to do with him and it was Karen who made a big fuss of him, but she wouldn't listen. In her mind I'd paid for the meal, so it was all my fault. If only she could have been there she would have seen how I showed no interest. I wouldn't give him the time of day. I just did what I felt I ought to do.

I think part of her anger was that she still really carried a torch for him. I'm convinced if he'd asked to come back she would have welcomed him. There was never really anyone else for her. She met a couple of blokes over the years, but she never had another serious relationship. When she did go out with anyone Karen used to be horrible to them, so that they soon disappeared. I used to say to Karen,

'Leave them alone. Let Mum get on with her life and find someone else,' but Karen didn't see it like that.

At the back of my mind is always the thought that I was to blame for the break-up of their marriage. I was the other man, and I took all my mum's energy and attention. She put everything into me, all her love and affection and care. My dad came second. I was her number one priority. It was maternal instinct, I guess, but that love was mutual. I think perhaps that was one of the problems for Shelagh and me. When someone loves and cares for you that much it is difficult for anyone else to take their place. I'm not saying that my mum was blind to my faults – for example, she wouldn't cover up for me if I was in the wrong – but she'd always protect me.

So 1996 was an eventful year, what with my dad turning up and Shelagh and me expecting our new arrival. We already knew the baby would be a girl. When we'd gone for the scan the doctor asked Hollie,

'What would you like? A little baby brother, or a little baby sister?'

Hollie said, 'A baby sister, please.'

The doctor said, 'Well, you've got your wish.'

I'd so longed for a boy, but I tried to hide my disappointment. I wasn't very successful, however, as during one of our volatile rows, I said to Shelagh,

'You couldn't even get that right.'

It was a terrible thing to say and it's haunted me ever since, especially as when Jessica was born I fell in love with her immediately and would do anything for her. I love both my girls to bits, and they will never want for anything while I am around to take care of them.

It was during that year also that I decided to bite the bullet, give up legal work and concentrate on my comedy career. I was juggling so much: the day job, the night work and the compensation campaign. Something had to give and I was getting tired of the legal work, while at the same time I was getting lots of comedy work and earning good money for it. However, as well as being involved in the legal aspects of our ongoing campaign against Diageo, I was still often called on to give legal advice to friends and acquaintances.

In April 1996 I was booked to appear at a club in Carlisle after their screening of the FA Cup Final between Manchester United and Liverpool. Because I wanted to see the match myself, I asked if I could arrive early, have lunch there and watch the match before I went on, and they happily agreed. Before the match there was a celebrity penalty shoot-out between former Liverpool and Man United players and I nearly choked on my roast beef and Yorkshire pudding when I saw the ex-Liverpool player Tommy Smith, one of my childhood heroes, take a winning shot and then do a fifty-yard triumphant run along the pitch.

My shock wasn't to do with hero-worship, though. It was because two years earlier I'd performed with Tommy at a sportsman's dinner, and it had been obvious that he was in severe pain and could hardly walk. I'd said to him then that he should be claiming Disability Living Allowance. He thought he wasn't eligible as he was still working on the after-dinner circuit, but then I explained that the rules for claiming the benefit didn't take account of earnings. I helped Tommy with filling in the forms and, to his surprise, he was awarded the benefit and was able to get a Motability car.

I hadn't seen him since then but a week or two after seeing him taking that penalty kick I got a phone call from him, irately demanding if I had told the DHSS that he was no longer entitled to the DLA.

'It must have been you,' he stormed. 'Nobody else would know about it.'

'Tommy,' I replied, 'Do you not think the fact that you took a penalty kick and ran up the pitch at the Cup Final in full view of six million viewers on national TV might have had something to do with it?'

'Do you think so?' was his reply, which left me lost for words.

What had happened was that the benefit officer who had processed Tommy's original application obviously remembered doing so, as Tommy was a celebrity. He too had been watching the match on TV that day. On his return to work the following Monday he'd immediately taken steps to have Tommy's benefit rescinded. The officer was only doing his job. His actions would have had nothing to do with the fact that he was a staunch Everton supporter.

Of course Tommy had to appeal. His grounds were that the football club had made sure he had special painkilling injections in his knees before he went out, to enable him to take the penalty, and I have no reason to disbelieve that. The appeal process dragged on for two years, with me assisting him and attending hearings. Of course the media had a field day with the whole thing. At the end of it we came out with a limited victory as Tommy's benefit was reinstated, but only at the lower rate of the mobility allowance.

Tommy seemed to think that I was somehow at fault in all that had happened to him. I felt that he thought I hadn't represented him competently, and wasn't doing my best for him. During the appeal period he had a bad car accident on the M58, was pulled out of the car by two passing workmen and had to wear a spinal cage for some time. At one hearing we attended a TV reporter covering the case told us that the two men who had got him out of the car were working round the corner, and suggested that it would make good television for Tommy to meet them. Tommy brushed him off, saying he hadn't got time. I'm afraid my hero-worship rather slipped as I got to know the real man. I used to bump into him now and again on the after-dinner circuit and I would be polite to him, but that is all.

Jessica was born on 5 January 1997, and again it was a huge relief that she was perfectly normal. However, she didn't seem to feed very well, and we had a lot of difficulty with her in the first few months. What we didn't know was that actually she'd been born with a cleft palate, and this remained undiagnosed until she was five years old. When we did find out it rang alarm bells for me. I remembered that cleft palate is a condition associated with thalidomide damage and it brought back to me William McBride's claim that thalidomide could cause genetic damage, which could result in inherited defects.

Me with Shelagh, Hollie and baby Jessica

We engaged Leigh Day & Co. with a view to claiming compensation for Jess, but eventually we dropped the case as Leigh Day advised us that there was no real evidence that cleft palate could be related to thalidomide damage and the condition is so common in the ordinary population. It still worries me, especially as Hollie developed ear problems, which is another condition often found as a result of thalidomide damage. I have warned them both that should they bear a child with any deformity at all they must take action against Diageo and whichever government is in power at the time.

At this point in time we knew only that we had another lovely daughter, and the problems in our marriage were smoothed over as we settled down to look after her. Meanwhile, Hollie had reached school age, and I had to do my share of the school runs. I would take Hollie down to the school gates in the car, but I wouldn't go in with her. I remembered how cruel kids had been to me when I was a schoolkid, and I didn't want Hollie to be teased or bullied on my account because of my appearance. I'd also piled on a lot of weight again, and that was another reason why I didn't want to be seen taking her into school.

Happy Days: Pictured with a young Jonathan Ross in 1997.

Still, life was generally good. The house extension was finished, Shelagh and the kids had everything they wanted and we were able to take nice holidays. Florida is one of my favourite places and, since our first visit in 1992, the first two weeks of every year were set aside for a family holiday in the Florida sunshine. It always was one of the few times in the year that I could relax and have fun with my family. Although Jessica was only a baby Hollie was getting to an age where she could really enjoy the trip and all the activities. I used to think I would love to retire to Florida if my health and financial position permitted it. But now, in 2015, I don't really know what life has in store for me.

It was around this time in the late 1990s that I had my first experience of working abroad. As I've said, I'd made a few friends in the comedy business. One of them is Alan Bates, a hypnotist from the Wirral. Alan was working out in the Middle East for the Sultan of Brunei when he met a Manchester DJ called Sharell at a party. Sharell was soon to move to Dubai and had a plan to put together a package of nightclub acts to include a hypnotist, an alternative stand-up and a mainstream stand-up. She wanted to call it 'The Laughter Factory'. The trouble was, she confided in Alan, that she didn't know a mainstream stand-up who would fit the bill.

'I know the very man,' said Alan, and told her about me. The first thing I knew about it was when Alan phoned me and asked me if I fancied working in the Middle East. Of course I jumped at the chance, and before I knew it I was on a plane heading for Dubai.

We played to full houses everywhere we went, even in the Dubai Country Club, where the squash court had been converted to a theatre to hold the audience. Sharell and her partner Duncan were excellent organisers, and they gained sponsorship from Martell brandy, Coca-Cola and Tom Thumb cigars. I took my old friend Jimmy Coulthard with me as my minder/carer, and we had a fabulous time working in Abu Dhabi, Dubai and Bahrain.

When we first arrived in Bahrain we were booked to work in the club below the Hotel Bison. The manager had arranged for us to stay in the hotel and, to our amazement, we were given a free bar tab. This seemed to be because the King of

Bahrain had expressed desire to meet us and was sending a chauffeur-driven limo to collect us the next morning and take us to his private beach. Of course we were all in the bar most of the night, and ended up completely drunk. The next morning we were all dead to the world, so missed the appointment. We only woke up at midday to find numerous notes shoved under the door from the hotel staff, who had been trying to wake us.

I had to go to the office and put a phone call through to the palace, apologising to the king's aides for not turning up. It was a massive mistake on my part. Apparently any interview with the king was likely to end with a generous gift, usually a Rolex Oyster. I was told because of my disability, that I was likely to receive something more ornate such as a diamond-encrusted dagger so I missed out on that. And I also missed the opportunity of having my photo taken with the King of Bahrain, which would have been excellent publicity for me. But that's life, and anyway I still had a marvellous time in the Middle East. I worked out there on four separate tours between 1998 and 2000, and will be permanently indebted to Sharell and to Alan Bates for such a happy experience.

There were dark undertones even then, with the club we worked on the last night in Bahrain reputedly being on the hit list for al-Qaeda. We were never actually threatened, but the presence of armed guards in the hotel corridors was sobering. That's the price of fame and stardom...

At home, despite having given up legal work, I seemed destined to be forever entangled in litigation. The campaign on behalf of Glen and Debbie Harrison fizzled out, and their legal aid certificate was eventually withdrawn. There just wasn't enough reliable evidence to sustain the claim of inherited thalidomide damage. We then decided to go back to Diageo to ask for a further top-up to the Trust Fund.

We knew we would have an even harder fight on our hands this time, as Diageo would obviously think that because they had already given us money in 1995 they should have no further liability. Mr Davidson, who had negotiated with us in 1995, had now left the company. We now had to deal with Geoffrey Bush and Murray Loake, who was the PR expert for Guinness. Our solicitors were Leigh Day & Co., who were experienced in compensation cases, including cases brought by British smokers and British prisoners of war in Japanese prison camps. Martin Day offered the firm's services gratis after seeing the thalidomide victim Kim Morton on television.

Shelagh and me with rugby league legend Alex Murphy,
one of the first of my collection of celebrity photos.

From previous experience I knew that Diageo would be reluctant to pay out (to put it mildly) unless they were being hit in the pocket, so I began to lay plans of my own.

My career brings me into contact with a lot of showbiz and sports personalities, and we all know the connection between sport and the consumption of alcohol for the average fan. Also, sports celebrities assume almost godlike significance for their fans, so that their endorsement of products is closely sought by manufacturers. We see them advertising not just sport-related items, but everything from crisps to aftershaves.

I've always found it easy to get on with people and make friends, and whenever I appear with someone famous (more famous than me, of course) I go out of my way to be photographed with them and make sure they will remember me.

Daily Post Friday 16 March 2000.
Reproduced by kind permission of
Trinity Mirror Newspapers/Liverpool
Echo and Daily Post.

Now my popularity was about to pay off. I began to approach people I knew who might be willing to support our campaign, and soon I had compiled a list of famous names. These included: Roy 'Chubby' Brown, Bernard Manning, Gordon Banks, Nobby Stiles, Martin Peters, the late Peter Osgood, Peter Bonetti, Michael Owen, Robbie Fowler, Jamie Redknapp and many others.

In my footballing days I once coached a team owned by Theo Constantino, a Greek millionaire who lived in Cheshire. During that time the team had a centre forward named

Robert Fowler, who I became quite friendly with. Robert had a four-year-old son, also named Robert, who grew up to be Robbie Fowler, best known for his career with Liverpool FC. I approached him and Steve McManaman and asked them to support our campaign. I was amazed and delighted to find that all five England internationals playing with Liverpool FC had signed forms stating that they would support a boycott of Diageo products if they did not enter into negotiations with us.

Shortly after this, in 1998, I was at a sportsman's dinner in the north-east where I met Brendan Ingle, who was then managing 'Prince' Naseem Hamed, a young boxer from Sheffield. Never one to miss an opportunity, I asked Brendan if we could engage 'Prince' Naseem's support for the campaign. He told me to come to the gym where Naseem trained and talk to him about it.

I had a gig in Sheffield soon after. I went early in the afternoon, and went to the gym where Naseem was expected. At first he was reluctant to talk to me, obviously wondering who I was and what I wanted, but after he'd spoken to Brendan he came and sat down with me once he'd finished his practice session. We shook hands and, from then on, we became good friends. I explained what I wanted but had to give him a potted history of what thalidomide and its producers had done to me and others like me, as being so young, he knew nothing about it.

He was quite horrified at the thought that Diageo and its predecessors had been so difficult regarding compensation, and exclaimed,

'Surely they can't be like this?'

I told him how the recent top-up was nowhere near enough, given the fact that there were 455 of us who were all getting older and incurring increasing care costs. Naz said he would help but it would be better to contact his brother who was better at administrative stuff, and he gave me his brother Riath's phone number, saying,

'Tell him I told you to phone and he'll do something for you, and I'll back it up.'

I thought he was just fobbing me off and said as much to Brendan, but Brendan said,

'If Naz promises to do something he will do it, and if he says his brothers will do it they will do it. You can trust him.'

Still, I went off to my gig with a bit of a heavy heart. I went down a bomb and felt better the next morning, but I still hesitated to ring Riath. I didn't want to be a pest, and I fully expected him to say he knew nothing about it. I finally rang about 11 am, and got the surprise of my life when he answered the phone and told me that Naz had rung him at nine o'clock and explained the story to him. I gave him more details, and he suggested that I write a sample statement of what I wanted them to say and that he would then modify it to suit them.

Fired with enthusiasm, I sat down and composed something that I thought would scare the daylights out of Diageo. I faxed it over to Riath who said he would sort it out in the next day or so but – to my surprise – it came back two hours later, and he had not just modified it but made it so much better than my original attempt.

Also to my surprise, Naz agreed to personally deliver the letter to Anthony Greener (the chairman of Diageo) at his office, and jokingly invited him down to the car park. My hopes were crushed when we got the reply, although it was really only what I should have expected. It basically said that they were not frightened by our tactics, and that there was no more money forthcoming. Obviously the Hamed brothers and I were disgusted with this arrogant response. At this rate the British thalidomiders would be in dire financial straits by 2009.

Freddie Astbury (left), Bernard Manning and me sadly contemplating the position of thalidomide victims during the 1999 campaign.

It was time to take off the velvet gloves. I'd made footage of all the celebrities who'd offered to support me. They all condemned Diageo's failure to treat us properly. Freddie Astbury was also once more on hunger strike, which added fuel to the gathering campaign. I contacted Geoffrey Bush of Diageo and he agreed to meet us, along with the rest of his PR team at a London hotel.

I'd also met Frankie Fraser, the famous underworld figure who was now a celebrity speaker on the after-dinner circuit, and he too agreed to support the campaign. I wasn't bothered about his notoriety. I could see how his influence in the East End could well wreak havoc on Diageo's sales in the area. I took Frankie along as part of our team, but the first thing Geoffrey Bush did in his opening speech was to remonstrate with me for allowing a convicted murderer to attend the meeting.

I'm always quick with my verbal responses but Frankie beat me to it, declaring in his distinctive cockney accent,

'Here, hang on a sec. I cut down a couple of arseholes in a gangland dispute. You bastards fucking murdered thousands of innocents. I did a couple of stretches of penance but your fucking lot got off fucking scot-fucking-free.'

There was absolute silence for a moment. Then Mr Bush carried on as if nothing had been said and the meeting got underway. Although there was a lot of talking and listening on both sides I came away with the feeling that nothing had been achieved, and the whole thing seemed to be an exercise in time-wasting.

Reproduced by kind permission of the
Daily Express/N&S Syndication.

Before the next meeting at the Novotel Hotel in Birmingham I was speaking at a dinner show where Paul Gascoigne was also on the bill. I intended to ask him to join our campaign as he was a major media celebrity at the time, but on the actual night he was unable to attend. However, his father was in the audience and assured me he would speak to Gazza, and that he was sure he would support us.

I informed Geoffrey Bush that we would have Gazza on our team. However, at our next meeting (after showing him the condemnatory video footage made by all the celebrities), he queried why Paul Gascoigne wasn't in the film.

Quick as a flash, I said, 'I'll bring him on as an impact player.'

Of course it wasn't strictly true as I still hadn't heard from Gazza, but desperate men do desperate things and I hoped it would do the trick for us. As Geoffrey Bush prepared to leave the meeting, I told him,

'Go away and think about making a meaningful offer to us, or I release all we have to the media tomorrow.'

He rang me about 11 pm that night and said, 'If you want to release the videos, go ahead. We're multinational, and your would-be all-stars don't frighten us.'

I now realised that I had to get hold of a maverick or two, some people who could make a difference to Diageo's share price. While this was dawning on me I was sitting watching the Sky Sports News coverage of Manchester United fans objecting to the takeover of the club by the American business family, the Glazers.

The old light bulb flashed in my head. On the back of the Manchester United news, what if I could arrange a press conference at Manchester City's stadium suggesting that Manchester City was also subject to a takeover, although this time, by two global celebrities and life-long fans of the club – Noel and Liam Gallagher?

I asked Mike Summerbee, a former Manchester City and England great, to introduce me to the Gallagher brothers.

Mike agreed to talk to them, and in no time at all they had called me. I hatched a plan to convince Diageo that a press conference at Manchester City's stadium was to take place with Noel and Liam Gallagher. The world media would be watching, as speculation that Oasis were about to buy the club would be the news of the day in both the UK and the United States.

I rang Geoffrey Bush at Diageo to invite him to attend

and to give him fair warning that when the press conference (which was scheduled for 2 pm, to ensure that viewers in the United States were up and watching) began, we would bring out Noel and Liam Gallagher with some of the most severe thalidomide damaged people in the UK... and rather than announcing a take-over, they would ask the world media to boycott Diageo's products.

The next day things took a very different turn. Geoffrey Bush rang me to say that Diageo were going to extend our covenant to 2022 (rather than the existing 2009) and that they would index-link it, as we had asked. He ended by warning me that this was a final offer. I said,

'Mr Bush, each and every time has been a final offer.'

I put the phone down and danced round the room. It was only a partial euphoria, though. We'd succeeded but only, really, in a small way. It still wasn't enough, but it was better than nothing.

The next day I was in trouble again, and my joy at victory was short-lived. I got a phone call from Neil Buckland at the Thalidomide Trust and his first words were,

'I don't know, Skyner. You're a fucking loose cannon. You've really upset the apple cart, and Diageo are not happy with you whatsoever. You know they've agreed to pay another twelve years on the covenant so I must give you credit for that, but the problem is they don't want you going about shouting how you made them do it. They want to show they were willing to do it anyway, and they want you to go along with that.'

It was a monumental cheek, but I didn't care about that. I only wanted to ensure that nothing jeopardised the Trust getting the money. I replied that I was happy to sing Diageo's praises, provided they showed that they would do the right thing and make proper provision for the UK thalidomiders.

Buckland went on to outline the Trust's position. This was,

basically, that they understood that Diageo realised that some of the beneficiaries were facing increasing health problems and so would require extra finance. Diageo were therefore willing to extend the covenant on the condition that any new monies paid from it would be given only to individuals whose conditions were deteriorating.

I was furious. Talk about moving the goalposts. I told Buckland,

'Neil, they are lying. Last night Bush told me they would pay the money unconditionally. You ring him back and tell him the deal's off, and I'm releasing all the videos because he's reneged on what he promised me.'

Buckland got me to calm down. He said he would speak to Bush and arrange for us to give a joint press statement. It would also be necessary for me to write a letter praising Diageo and thanking them for doing the right thing. He said that if I did this he felt sure they could sort out the business about the money and who it was paid to later. The important thing was that we secured the payment in the first place.

I wanted to refuse, but I could see his point. Under pressure I agreed and, though it rankled, wrote the letter as asked. The covenant was set up that year, with the agreement to pay £2.5 million index-linked till 2022.

So at the end of 2000 I felt we were sitting pretty. The extra money would make a big difference to the Trust, and provide some security for its beneficiaries. But nothing ever seems to turn out quite as you expect. Great changes were imminent. The first was that Neil Buckland left the Thalidomide Trust and the directorship was taken over by Dr Martin Johnson. The second had a more far-reaching effect and a more distant source in the Middle East with al-Qaeda.

Chapter 11

After 9/11

Dr Martin Johnson spent twenty-one years in the RAF, first as a pilot who fought in the Falklands War and then as an administrative officer and a NATO intelligence specialist. After leaving the RAF he worked as a financial and management advisor, and before joining the Thalidomide Trust he had spent six years as CEO of a children's hospice.

Dr Martin Johnson of the Thalidomide Trust

On taking up directorship of the Trust, the first task Johnson set himself was to visit every single beneficiary. Although most of these visits were completed in the first eighteen months of his tenure it took him ten years to accomplish the task, as some of the UK thalidomiders were now living as ex-pats in countries as far away as China.

I was one of the first to be visited, and when he came to see me the first thing he asked was my opinion of the Trust. In view of my past experiences I had plenty to say on the matter, and I'm not one for mincing my words. I told him how I felt I had been unfairly assessed and treated. I felt that the Trust had always danced to the tune of DCBL/Guinness/Diageo rather than standing up for us thalidomiders. I also explained how I thought the Establishment had created the conditions for thalidomide to be marketed with such dreadful results in the first place, and how it had connived to delay justice and minimise compensation and that it continued to do so. I finished by saying,

'I'm convinced that the Trust is part of this set-up and, as director of the Trust, so also are you.'

I was only beginning to get on my hobby horse but he stopped me right there, saying,

'I'm sorry you see it that way, Gary. I have been looking at your file and I want to reassure you that now I'm in charge we will operate with total transparency. I hope to change your opinion of both the Trust and myself.'

To demonstrate this transparency he offered to leave my file with me so I could examine it but I was so impressed by his apparent sincerity that it seemed mistrustful to accept the offer and I said,

'No, it's OK, as long as you accept now that I haven't been telling lies about what's happened to me.'

It wasn't actually such a huge concession, as the Freedom of Information Act had just gained royal assent and was partly implemented in November 2000. However, with hindsight, I should have hung on to the file as later – when I did want to access it – there were some problems. If I'd kept it at home I could have gone through its often startling contents at leisure and copied the relevant documents.

Before he left Johnson asked if I was in need of anything, and I brought up the subject of a kitchen extension we wanted and also floated the idea of getting a new car. To my surprise, he agreed without quibble. After he'd gone I grew a bit suspicious, especially regarding his easy agreement to my request for the extension loan. Was he just humouring me in an effort to curtail my activities as a loose cannon or giving me a payoff to keep me quiet? I voiced my concern to Shelagh but she told me to stop being paranoid, pointing out that whatever the Trust did I was suspicious. They were in a no-win situation where I was concerned.

I took what she said on board. Maybe this Dr Johnson really would sweep in a new era of cooperation with the beneficiaries. A sort of honeymoon period ensued between the Trust and me. I was delighted when, true to Johnson's word, I received a £35,000 loan in 2001 for the extension. Shortly after that he phoned me to say that he had now interviewed many Trust beneficiaries, and he could see that a lot of people besides me had been underassessed.

Don't forget that the allowances paid to beneficiaries were still based on the original assessments made in the 1970s. There had been no ongoing reassessment processes to allow for deteriorating conditions and increasing care needs. Johnson therefore proposed to set up individual reviews for beneficiaries to assess our present condition compared to our original assessments. Obviously this would require a lot of administrative work so he suggested that a friend of his, Alan Summerside, could carry out the task in a voluntary capacity alongside his paid job as an IT consultant with the Ministry of Defence.

This seemed a good idea to me, and Alan ended up staying at my house occasionally. We looked after him well and tried to make him feel at home, but I never really took to him. Alan was interested in getting a job at the Trust, and he told me that if he was successful he wanted to set up an employment scheme for thalidomiders. It would be called Enablers, something along the lines of Remploy. It sounded like a great idea, so when Dr Johnson asked if I would recommend Alan for a paid position to the Trustees I was happy to do so. My recommendation would carry some weight as I had been so prominent in the campaigns against Diageo, and in particular because it coincided with Johnson's recommendation.

Alan Summerside

So Alan was duly appointed. And then he was no longer staying with us but moved down closer to the Trust offices in Huntingdon, so I saw little of him from then on. The plan was for the Enablers employment scheme to be run by a community enterprise called McSence, which was based in Scotland. It was formed in 1988 to provide employment opportunities for communities and groups whose traditional employment bases – such as working in the mines, at the steelworks or at the docks – had disappeared, leaving them unable to support themselves. A project in partnership with Diageo and the Thalidomide Trust went ahead and provided employment for a percentage of thalidomiders.

Another good thing that came out of employing Alan was that he found documents in my file dated 1991 which showed that Trust officials had previously debated the low level of my allocation but had done nothing about it. As a result of this discovery Johnson told me they were going to upgrade me and backdate the increase to 1991, which would give me a back payment of £39,000. He clearly thought I would be delighted with this and I was, but it still wasn't right and I'm a stickler for fairness. I pointed out that if I was in the wrong band in 1991 I'd obviously been in the wrong band ever since 1972, when the assessment had been made, so I should be reimbursed back to that date.

Johnson dug his heels in, saying that the Trust's position was that they only had documentary evidence dating back to 1991, so that would have to be the base date for reassessment. The honeymoon was over, and war broke out between the Trust and me. As always, I was determined not to back down. An extended battle ensued where even the Trust chairman Sir Michael Wright got involved, and wrote to me personally. I engaged a series of lawyers, but with little success. I felt that they didn't really understand the issues involved. It dragged on for years, and cost a fortune. On top of that I had to repay the loan for the new extension, so I think I ended up with about £4,000.

This personal battle, however, was interrupted by the catastrophic events of 9/11. I was doing my accounts in the kitchen when I saw it on TV. I thought it was an action film till I heard them say it was breaking news. Then my accountant phoned me up about my accounts and he said,

'Have you seen what's going on?'

'Is it for real?' I said to him, 'This is the start of the fucking Third World War.'

I thought the US was bound to respond drastically to whoever was responsible, but of course at that time no one knew who was responsible. But there and then I thought that for all of us it wasn't going to be very long. I thought it was the end of the world. The fact that that didn't happen – that there was no instant retaliation – puzzles me.

Obviously that restraint saved the world from a horrendous war, but it does make me wonder if there is something in the conspiracy theories which argue that the United States were not completely innocent as regards the events of that day. Obviously there were a lot of financial effects for ordinary people as stocks and shares crashed – and, specifically, for the Thalidomide Trust, which relies on income from investments to protect payments to its beneficiaries. That's why the Trust had to get involved in a new campaign for more money.

In the original settlement with DCBL everyone had thought that as the Trust was set up as a charity it would be exempt from income tax. But in 1974 the Inland Revenue declared that payments to thalidomide victims should be treated as income, and therefore subject to income tax. The families who'd already accepted a low settlement were horrified, and disaster was only averted when MP Jack Ashley persuaded the government to pay £5 million into the Trust fund to offset the tax cost. These government top-ups continued up until 1996, regardless of which party was in power, while the Trust continued to be forced to pay tax. It seems a farcical situation, but nevertheless millions of pounds intended for Trust fund beneficiaries went into the coffers of HMRC.

In 2002 Gordon Brown, then Chancellor of the Exchequer, announced that because of the award of £32.5 million pounds made to the Trust in 2000 the Trust could afford to pay its taxes, and therefore the payments from the government would be discontinued. By this petty action the government put Britain in the unenviable position of being the only country to directly tax its thalidomide citizens; the only country to make a profit from their disabilities. In the Republic of Ireland the Irish Taxes Consolidation Act of 1997 even goes so far as to specifically stipulate tax exemption for thalidomide victims.

It was a terrible blow on top of the financial devastation

wreaked by 9/11. Of course our response was to take up the campaign again, this time aimed at changing the government's decision. A two-pronged attack was mounted. Firstly, our small but determined band of soldiers in the Thalidomide Action Group began applying pressure in our usual unorthodox ways. In December 2002 I wrote to Gordon Brown stating our intention to shame the government with a massive poster campaign, as follows:

Dear Mr Brown,

Re: Thalidomide

I write to advise you that an adjournment debate will take place in the House this coming Monday 9 December 2002, tabled by Jonathan Djanogly MP, regarding the above and the tax liabilities placed on thalidomide sufferers by this and previous governments.

It is important that you understand that we are very determined for you to change your stance with regard to our tax position. If you fail to listen to and then to act on our requests, we have 207 poster sites in the North West that will carry a huge poster of Michael Owen, David Beckham and Robbie Fowler, alongside three thalidomide victims in wheelchairs. The slogan on the poster will say NEW LABOUR TAX THESE SIX PEOPLE AT THE SAME RATE – HOW CAN YOU VOTE FOR A PARTY THAT DOES THIS?

I hope this campaign is not necessary but you have to understand we thalidomide folk have put up with second rate compensation for forty-odd years and not even had the courtesy of an apology and it's about time we were treated properly instead of the lies and lip service we have had from you and all previous governments.

I look forward to your response.

Yours sincerely

Gary Skyner.

As usual the government stuck its head in the sand, hoping we would go away, but at the same time another attack was being launched by two other thalidomiders, Nick Dobrik and Guy Tweedy. They campaigned tirelessly on behalf of the British thalidomiders to get the tax abolished, lobbying MPs, lords and other thalidomiders. They were involved in over 2,500 interviews between 2002 and 2004. During these years I was mostly working away on the Spanish costas, and it was while there on 20 July 2004 that I heard that the government had finally agreed to remove the tax on the Trust fund.

I thought then we could relax at last. The 2000 settlement from Diageo plus the tax exemption should have secured all our futures but you never know what is round the corner, and soon we were back on the campaign trail. At this point, however, I was busy expanding my comedy career into international territory.

I'd been working with the agent Tony Jacobs for some years, and through this had developed a good following in the north-east. In 2002 Tony fell ill with cancer and sadly died in the October of that year, but some months beforehand he was thinking of moving to Spain and tried to persuade his partner to do so. The Benidorm scene was very big at that time. It was a really popular year-round holiday resort for Brits. The booze was cheap, people went on ciggy runs to get cheap fags and the resort catered to the British with English-style food, Brit-style pubs and, of course, British entertainers.

One of the top comics was Geordie comedian Ned Kelly, who spent two or three months over there every year, but in the end he got tired of playing Benidorm and asked Tony Jacobs if I'd be interested in taking his place.

Now as a young man I'd never been able to do the gap year or the backpacking stuff that young people do because of my disability, but I've always loved travelling abroad and the stint in Dubai had given me a taste for more.

Tony and I went out on a sort of trial. I was booked to do the famous Steptoes I club. As usual I was pretty confident but the first night was a terrible experience. I died on my arse and virtually emptied the club… all in front of the watchful gaze of the managers, Pepe and Antonio. When I retreated to my dressing room to lick my wounds Pepe came in and told me he could see I was a good comic, but my style and delivery were all wrong for Benidorm.

'Come in tomorrow and watch how the other guys do it,' was his advice.

I wasn't used to taking criticism or advice. I was used to being fêted back home, and hadn't I been voted Merseyside King of Comedy three years running? Who was this bloke to come and tell me I was doing it all wrong? But I didn't want a repeat performance like that and in my heart I could tell he knew what he was on about, so the next night I watched Billy Fontaine and Danny Downing wow their audiences. It was a different style to mine: much slower, with fewer jokes and more chatting to the crowd. It seemed a bit of a cheat to me, but if that's what they wanted…

I was OK after that and worked regularly at Steptoes I and II, but I soon realised that the sun, sea and booze lifestyle on the costas wasn't all it was cracked up to be. The heat can be relentless, especially when you're working rather than lazing about on the beach. You eat rubbish most of the time, work through most of the night and try to sleep in the day… and the place is full of people just getting pissed out of their minds.

Shelagh and the kids came along for some of the trips, but I only got accommodation costs for myself. We were eating out all the time and the pay wasn't that good in the clubs to start with, so I seemed to be out of pocket a lot of the time. Even when the family wasn't along I still had to have a carer with me, who had to be paid at my own expense.

Hollie and Jessica enjoying the sun in Benidorm in 2003.

Eventually, with the help of another loan from the Thalidomide Trust, I decided to buy an apartment out there. The first place I saw was really nice. It had lovely furniture and everything, and the owner was selling at a reasonable price because her husband had died and she wanted to return to England. I wanted to jump at it, but in my mind I could see my Grandma Skyner wagging her finger at me and saying,

'There you go, impetuous Harry. First thing you see, you got to have, without looking at all the others.' I left it, looked at some other places and got talked into buying this apartment just outside Benidorm.

It turned out to be a nightmare. It was one of those jerry-built places where the doors don't fit and the plumbing never works properly. During the times when I wasn't working in Spain I used to let the place out, but then there were the usual tenant problems. There were people moving in and out all the time, and it's impossible to keep an eye on what's going on from such a distance. One time I arrived from England to find the existing tenant filling up a van with half the furniture. If I hadn't turned up the place would have been totally stripped.

I stopped working regularly in Benidorm in 2005. I'm not saying there weren't some good times, but the novelty wore off. I realised it wasn't a healthy lifestyle for me, and I knew I could probably make a better living at home. The atmosphere on the club circuit in Benidorm wasn't good because other performers tried to pinch your gags. They don't like you if you're popular, and do their best to slag you off or just ignore you. I'm used to working among friends and getting on with everyone, so I really didn't like it. There were disagreements and rivalry among club owners and managers too. If you worked for one club they didn't like you gigging somewhere else on other nights. You felt as if you had to watch your back all the time.

On top of all that the Spanish bonanza was running down. Prices were going up and the sunseekers were heading off to cheaper resorts in Turkey and Bulgaria, where booze and food cost very little. The final straw for me came when the two Steptoe clubs closed down in the recession.

I've been back to Benidorm a couple of times, just to work a few days, but I'd never go back on a regular basis. The lifestyle just doesn't suit me. Sometimes, when they were stuck for an act, they would ring me up and I'd say,

'What are you paying?' and they'd say something like,

'It's 130 euros, and you pay for your own flight and taxi.'

One club owner told me to get the bus. Me on the bus with a suitcase? You can guess what my reply was.

I suppose Benidorm was good for me in that it furthered my career and got my face known but, on the other hand, I had some of my worst nights in the resort's clubs. There were some terrible audiences and that didn't help my reputation at all. People would say to their friends,

'Oh, I saw Gary Skyner in Liverpool last week. He was great,' and the friends might say back,

'Oh, really? I don't think so. I saw him in Benidorm, and

he was rubbish.' So working in Benidorm can damage your health.

Anyway, I had other fish to fry back home. Around this time I got a message from Ricky Tomlinson inviting me to appear with him at an event featuring Ken Dodd. I hadn't seen Ricky for several years. We'd been quite friendly while he was still on the comedy circuit, but then he got into *Brookside* and *The Royle Family*, so I was quite surprised when he contacted me. It rekindled our friendship, and I've worked with him quite a few times since then.

Me and Ricky Tomlinson

I was still doing lots of club work. *Never turn anything down*, that's my motto, and unless you've worked the place before you never know what kind of venue you are being sent to. At the same time I was developing a reputation on the after-dinner circuit, which required quite a different style of approach. It was more toned down than my club routine.

It was at one of these after-dinner speeches that I got talking to Steve Kindon, who used to be a star footballer for Burnley and Wolverhampton Wanderers. He told me he was getting into motivational speaking to big businesses, and he used analogies about teamwork in football to motivate employees in the corporate sector.

I thought to myself, *If he can make money doing that… Surely my story is even more dramatic. Following the biggest medical disaster in history I have a true life story to tell about turning adversity into success against all odds, and I'm a living testament to that success story.*

I set about carefully preparing material and advertising myself as a motivational speaker. The first booking I got was for the Nationwide Building Society and I was scared stiff but I got through it, and after that my reputation developed. So motivational speaking is now a regular part of my work, and one that I greatly enjoy.

Of course there are lots of other motivational speakers. Many of them are much more famous than I am, but many of these are famous because of some special gift, usually athletic. They are mountain climbers or Olympic athletes, whose vision and determination has spurred them on to achieve the highest goals. I like to think I'm different because I started with a handicap, not a gift, but have turned it to my advantage in order to live a full and interesting life.

Motivational speaking at Chilterns College, High Wycombe, 2011.

I got some media publicity when I was asked to appear regularly on a BBC Radio Merseyside show called *Roger's*

Panel, which was hosted by the popular presenter Roger Phillips. The show featured discussions of topical issues. I'd have to select items that interested me from the day's news and then talk about them on air with Roger. I was expected to take an opposing view to what Roger said in order to stimulate listeners to ring up and participate in the debate. At first the producers were worried that I might dry up on air. Obviously they didn't know me. With my big mouth and the gift of the gab there was no chance of that. The show ran for quite some time, and I really enjoyed doing it. I didn't get paid, but it was good fun and good publicity for me.

In 2004 I achieved another major ambition when I got my pilot's licence, largely just to prove to myself I could do it. Long before 9/11 I flew to Dubai to work with a mate Alan Bates, as I have mentioned before. One of the stewards on the plane took a shine to him, and asked if he'd like to come and see the cockpit. Alan was a bit dubious about the guy's motives as he was obviously gay, so he insisted that I be allowed to go along too. It wouldn't happen now, but in those days things were a bit more relaxed. In the cockpit was the pilot, the navigator and a checker. They recognised me from my photo in a magazine they'd been reading while waiting for take-off. It was an article about my comedy work in the Middle East.

They asked about the show I was going to do, and said that as they were going to be staying down there for three days they would like to come and see my act. They weren't allowed to drink for forty-eight hours before flying back, so they only really had that night to enjoy themselves. We organised it all for them – free entry and a free bar – and rang their hotel, and four of them turned up and had a really good time. They were just really nice ordinary blokes.

When we turned up at Dubai airport to go home we were in the departure lounge watching the plane through the windows, and we could see these guys waving to us from the nose and trying to tell us something. The next thing was that someone came to fetch us and took us on board before everybody else and put us in club class. We had our own beds and everything. We were well impressed, but there was another treat in store. We were allowed to sit up front for take-off, so we sat on the jump seats in the cockpit.

The plane went down the runway and there was this huge bank of red, white and green lights. Then they got the go-ahead from control. One turned to the other and said,

'Shall we go, then?' just like they were driving a bus or something, and off we went. I was hooked from that moment. I said to myself,

'I've got to fucking do this.'

But it was a big downer, getting in a Cessna, when I eventually did get to fly myself. I talked about it for a while and mentioned it to Shelagh, and on my forty-second birthday I got a voucher for a two-hour training flight. After that I took more lessons. I just loved it.

I had a problem changing over the fuel tanks as I had to lean down to reach and nearly took the plane into a dive. The trainer yelled at me,

'What the fuck are you doing? You can't do that.'

So I had to get an adaptation that would allow me to work the controls without losing control, but it was great and I was determined to succeed. I remember thinking as I flew how my dad used to put me down and say I wouldn't be able to do things. I felt a savage satisfaction in passing that exam, and I was delighted when BBC TV made a documentary about it.

The documentary was really about all us thalidomiders and how we had fared during our lives, but when they heard about my flying lessons they wanted to cover that. It was a problem because the producer wanted to come up and film me flying, but it wasn't allowed under the civil aviation authority rules. My trainer made a concession and allowed them to fly with us, and the producer was sitting in the back and she puked up. We were flying over Liverpool, and we got permission to buzz the two football grounds. I'm a Liverpudlian and the trainer was an Evertonian, and I was going,

'We want to be over here,' and swerving the plane over Anfield and then he'd go,

'No, we want to be over here,' and he'd swerve over Everton's ground, and we kept doing that for a bit and then we realised she was sitting behind us with a blanket over her head. She had an all-black top on, and when we got off the plane she had a big stain down the front where she'd puked up.

I wonder if my dad ever saw the programme. I'd had little contact with him since that visit in 1996, and he never sent any birthday or Christmas cards to any of us. One year I saw a birthday card in a shop and the message on the front read: *To my dad – you were always a helping hand*. I bought it and wrote inside,

'If only the sentiments on the front of this card were true.' I sent it to him for his birthday but I never got a response. I never heard anything from him for years after that.

The years when I was mostly working abroad and developing new career opportunities were a welcome change to the constant backdrop of thalidomide and the campaign for compensation. After the 2000 settlement I'd hoped that would be the end of it and that I could now get on with my life, but there seemed to be no end to the thalidomide story. I've already detailed how, despite the terrible tragedy of thousands of deformed children, thalidomide has been successfully used in the treatment of leprosy and AIDS. It seemed that the drug was an effective treatment for a number of autoimmune diseases, and research at the beginning of the twenty-first century was investigating thalidomide as a possible treatment for certain cancers – notably myeloma.

They say it's an ill wind that blows nobody any good, and

despite the damage to myself and countless others I felt that if thalidomide could prove effective in saving lives then I was happy for it to be used – although, like most thalidomiders, I had misgivings about the possibilities of more deformed children being born as a result.

Was it possible that thalidomide could be rendered harmless and harnessed for the good of human health? I didn't know, but what I did know was that thalidomide was still a profitable drug for its inventors and producers. I also knew that by 2005, five years after the last Diageo top-up to British thalidomiders, we were sliding once more towards financial hardship thanks to the losses caused by 9/11. It seemed that the action group would have to take up the cudgels yet again, yet this time I found myself left out in the cold.

Chapter 12

'You Could Do With Losing a Bit of Weight'

The early years of the twenty-first century showed a consolidation of the Thalidomide Trust's move towards a more active role in negotiation for more compensation for its beneficiaries. In the past the Trust had seemed reluctant to participate in active campaigning. However, the formation of the National Advisory Council, which had been set up to assist the Trust in policy development and strategy, meant that they now had a more structured approach to the needs of thalidomiders and planning for their future. Members of the NAC are elected from the body of Trust members, so are well placed to advise the Trust itself on those needs and what needs to be done.

The realisation that the financial chaos that followed 9/11 had wiped out much of the benefit of the previous Diageo top-up led to further negotiations with the drinks company in 2005. These negotiations were led by Nick Dobrik and Guy Tweedy. Freddie Astbury was also involved, but I was sidelined. This was probably, I think, due to my reputation as a loose cannon.

I'd had the £39,000 backdated payment in 2002, and after that it seemed I was expected to be grateful and keep quiet. But, as I've already said, I didn't see it like that. Because I kept on insisting that I was owed money backdated to 1972 I was granted an individual beneficiary review in 2005. I had the impression that the review would be a formality, and would just go through without any problems. Nick Dobrik came with me in the role of an individual beneficiary review chaperone. In other words he was there as a fellow thalidomider to ensure that I stated my case properly and was fairly treated at the review, which was conducted by Alan Summerside in the October of 2005 at the American Library in London.

In December I was told that the panel had decided that there was no more money for me. I rang Martin Johnson, who confirmed the decision, saying that they had done everything by the book. I immediately contacted Nick Dobrik and told him what had happened, expecting him to support me in an appeal against the decision. He refused to do so, saying that as far as he was concerned the review had been fairly conducted. When I tried to speak to him about it further he ignored my calls and refused to answer the phone.

This made me very angry, as I felt as if I had been called a liar. It created a lot of bad blood between the Trust and me. And so, when the new campaign got going and they were writing letters to the MPs, I was just left out of it.

That was OK with me. I knew they wanted to act in a politically correct manner even though, in my opinion, past experience had shown that provocation and fear of losing public face were what was needed to make the machine cough up. It was an irreconcilable difference between the Trust and me. I can't help being a bull at the gate, but in my view the other side is always playing a waiting game. It can't be disputed that each year – as thalidomiders get older – a few more die off, which means that less money has to be paid out.

However, as a result of these new negotiations, agreement was reached with Diageo that same year for a further top-up of a special one-off payment of £4.4 million plus an increase in the annual payment from £2.8 million to £6.5 million. This would be index-linked, to cover the period to 2037. The negotiations were agreed in July, but the formal announcement didn't come till the December.

Of course I was pleased at the news but it still wasn't anywhere near enough to provide for future health needs, and it did rankle that I'd been left out of the negotiations after all the work I'd put in on earlier campaigns. But then I had a life beyond the Trust, so I just put it all behind me and got on with living.

Both my girls were growing up. Hollie left school and took a course in childcare.

Hollie and Jessica at Anfield.

Jessica was only eight but they were both keen football supporters, like their dad, so we had that in common. Jessica was also, like me, a good swimmer. She was like a little frog. Hollie had been afraid of water when she was smaller, yet also grew to be a confident swimmer. When we had the apartment in Benidorm there was a pool on the complex, so they got lots of practice.

My mission in life was to see they had everything they

wanted, and it was the same with Shelagh. If she wanted something I would make sure she got it, no matter how hard I had to work for it. Nothing but the best was good enough for them. We had a nice house in the pleasant Mossley Hill district of Liverpool and holidays to Florida when I could spare the time.

Shelagh and me on one of our many Florida holidays.

Looking back, maybe it wasn't the best thing to do – giving the kids everything they wanted, I mean. Sometimes there was jealousy from other kids who didn't have as much, and when Hollie left school she had her own car – which didn't go down well with some of her friends and workmates. I suppose that they were so used to getting what they asked for that they thought nothing of it and didn't always appreciate things, but they were the apples of my eye. I'd spent a lot of my early life wondering if I'd ever marry and if I'd be able to have kids. So, despite the fights Shelagh and I had, I still felt a lucky man to have my family.

Maybe it didn't help, either, that Shelagh never really had a separate life outside our home. Her time seemed to be taken up with looking after me and the girls and running the house. Even though I've achieved so much in my life I still need help with personal care on a daily basis and she was always there. She was a great mum and carer.

My mum used to go mad, saying I'd spoilt the kids, and that as they got older they should have been helping out at home – which they were never made to do. I tended to agree with Mum about that, especially when they were both teenagers, so that caused a lot more rows at home. But we still managed to get along.

Of course, I was away nearly every weekend. I'd usually have gigs Fridays, Saturdays and Sundays, often in quite different parts of the country, so by the time you added in driving time, I wouldn't get home till the early hours and I'd be dead on my feet. On weekdays there would be more time for family life, especially as I was no longer involved in campaigning, but I still needed to keep myself in the public eye. Developing a public profile and promoting my career also took up time.

In 2007 I was much saddened to learn that my long-term mate George Devlin had died, although it hardly came as a surprise. On Cup Final Day in 2006 he turned up at my house blind drunk at ten thirty in the morning, ostensibly to watch the match between Liverpool and West Ham. Our Jessica was home and at first she thought it was funny and was giggling at George's behaviour. But after a while she became frightened and it was very awkward, so it was almost a relief when he passed out on the sofa. Of course, he never saw the match. He was unconscious the whole time.

When I saw the state he was in I knew in my heart he wouldn't be able to go on much longer, but I tried to help him. I tried to get him to stay at mine for a few days so I could keep an eye on him, but he'd say he was coming and then not turn up. I was dead busy workwise so I couldn't keep track of him, but I was devastated when he died. I felt as if I owed him so much.

I thought that the reason his marriage failed was because

he was spending so much time with me. I suppose, really, if it was going to happen it was going to happen. I just felt that I was to blame because he doted on me so much. He was star-struck in a way.

I took him to a club in Stockport one night and I died on my arse. There were only about sixteen people in there, and it was clear that the audience was a bunch of deadheads. I had George staying at our house, and when we got home he said,

'It's a shame, lad, that you've lost it.'

I said, 'You fucking what?'

He said, 'It's a shame you've lost it. You were good at one time.'

I was speechless. The night after that we went to Blackpool and there were 350 people in the audience and I went down a bomb. I came off stage and George said,

'Fucking hell, I was wrong.'

I said, 'You were pissed. You weren't thinking straight.'

He looked after me when both my daughters were born and in those first years we were just like brothers. We did everything together. He was about five years older than me. I still miss him.

In 2008 I sold the apartment in Spain. It had become something of an albatross round my neck, and I'd already decided to avoid working abroad and to try to develop a career in motivational speaking.

In 2009 one of the most important people from my childhood years, John Smith Sr., came back into my life. In earlier chapters I've recounted how he became a surrogate dad to me. He filled the gap my own father left, along with my Grandpa Skyner.

Over the years I hadn't seen much of him, but in 2009 I bumped into him again. He came to a curry night at the Blenheim, one of the pubs I go to. I was planning a holiday to Florida with a few good mates and I invited John along. From there our friendship was rekindled. It seemed almost as if he was fated to come back into my life at that point because, as my married life deteriorated, he took on more and more the role of dear friend and close confidant as well as helping me with personal care.

Pals reunited: Me with John Smith Snr taking up where we left off.

With the new covenant between Diageo and the Trust all seemed fairly quiet on the thalidomide front. However, following on from this success, Dobrik and Tweedy (under the banner of the Trust's NAC) were mounting a campaign directly against Grünenthal and also against the UK government for a state payment to help the now ageing UK thalidomiders. Of course, I was left out of this and nothing much seemed to be happening. Unlike me, their approach was to do things by the book and through endless meetings and letters. In my opinion this usually results in a game of strategy between both sides, as both sides are practised in negotiation and delay.

However, thalidomide was still making news on the world scene. Already in use as a treatment for leprosy and for certain stages of HIV, the drug was being trialled in the US for treatment of multiple myeloma. In May 2006 the FDA granted approval for its use in this respect under the brand name Thalomid, which was manufactured by the Celgene Corporation. Because of the drug's terrible history great care was necessary to avoid more tragic birth defects. A mandatory programme STEPS (System for Thalidomide Education and Prescribing Safety) was introduced, to make all concerned aware of the dangers. Further trials were also required to demonstrate the drug's efficacy in treating multiple myeloma.

So thalidomide was gaining some respectability. Perhaps its creators, Chemie Grünenthal, thought the dreadful episode of 1958–62 could be put behind them and erased from the public memory. There was no chance of that while we, the living evidence, continued to survive. Maybe it seemed that the British thalidomiders were doing quite well, our futures secured by the latest agreement with Diageo, but these were uncertain times. To my mind, and probably to the minds of many others like me, doling out an allowance seemed like an insult. I felt I had never been properly compensated for the damage done to me and of course I still burnt with rage at the thought that, worldwide, Chemie Grünenthal had escaped virtually scot-free.

Because thalidomide had been manufactured under licence by pharmaceutical companies in many different countries, these companies were held responsible when it came to compensation claims, rather than Grünenthal. Grünenthal never made any attempt to shoulder the compensation burden in such countries and only made payments in countries where the company itself had been the sole distributor, such as in the Republic of Ireland.

Thalidomiders in these countries came off badly in terms of compensation, as Grünenthal's payments were miniscule in comparison to the damage done. In Germany the major contribution has come from the German government. Compensation schemes varied wildly from country to country. In some countries, such as Spain, thalidomide damage has never been officially recognised, and thus no compensation was ever paid.

However, thalidomiders the world over share the position of increasing health needs with advancing age. They also share a global financial position, where allowances and pensions shrink with fluctuating economic situations. From the 1990s on, with the development of the World Wide Web and improving information systems, communication channels and information exchanges were forming between groups of thalidomiders in different countries.

In 2007 discussions between the UK Thalidomide Trust and similar organisations in Germany led to the formation of the European Forum for Congenital Limb-Reduction Deficiencies, later renamed the European Dysmelia Reference and Information Centre. At the same time the NAC had announced its intention to pursue a claim against Chemie Grünenthal and, following a press announcement about this, the *Financial Times* reporter Andrew Jack secured an interview with Sebastian Wirtz, senior executive of the company and the grandson of the original founder.

When quizzed about the firm's responsibility for the thalidomide disaster Wirtz followed the line maintained by Chemie Grünenthal throughout the years. This was namely that the state of clinical knowledge at the time meant they had no way of knowing that thalidomide was teratogenic. In other words, he still refused to accept responsibility for what the company had done. Despite this, when questioned further on the company's moral duty to pay more compensation, he did make vague statements indicating that the firm was considering making 'a gesture' (Jack, 2007), whatever that might mean.

It wasn't going to wash. Thalidomide survivors had had fifty years to mull over Chemie Grünenthal's behaviour and to evaluate its attitude towards redressing the damage it had done. In Jack's article Nick Dobrik is quoted as saying,

'With Diageo we just had to put the pistol on the table. With Grünenthal we'll have to shoot three times in the head first.' (Jack, op. cit.)

In April 2008 the new British campaign was launched. It asked for £3 billion from the German government and Chemie Grünenthal jointly. Chemie Grünenthal's response was that it would not acknowledge any basis for the demands of the campaign. It was generally thought that a successful claim against the company would take years – given that there was any chance of success in the first place, which many doubted. The NAC and the Thalidomide Trust hedged their bets and continued their campaign against the UK government.

The government's attitude towards thalidomiders had always been ambivalent. Its early position had been that compensation was a matter for private litigation between the families and the supplier of the drug, but it had acknowledged some responsibility by inputting funds to offset tax liabilities and in 2004 had abolished the tax liability altogether. Encouraged by this step, the NAC redoubled their efforts to persuade the government to make some financial provision for the survivors. But they didn't seem to be getting anywhere very fast.

As I said, I'd been kept out of negotiations for fear that I might rock the boat. But in February 2009, following an early day motion requesting that the government set up a compensation scheme for thalidomiders and subsequent requests in Parliament for such a scheme (this was initiated by Jack Ashley), I wrote the following letter to Lord Darzi, the Under Secretary of State in the Department of Health:

Dear Lord Darzi,
Please allow me to introduce myself. My name is Gary Skyner;
I was the second born thalidomide victim in Great Britain, a
tragedy of which I am sure you are well aware, due to your
position in the House of Lords.

Late last week, it was brought to my attention, comments that you made in the House with regard to the status of the remaining 457 thalidomide victims and their increased needs for financial assistance and medical expertise from the Department of Health.

Can I ask you, have you ever in your life had the indignity of having to ask a third party to clean your backside after moving your bowels? Have you ever had the indignity of having a third party place you in the bath and had them clean you from head to toe? Have you ever visited a theme park and been a bigger attraction to the visitors than the actual themed events, because of your physical appearance?

Well, Sir, these are just a few of the indignities that I, as one person, have suffered throughout my life. There are many, many more. You can imagine how incensed I felt, reading your comments over the internet where you appear to be intimating that thalidomide victims are living in a land of milk and honey! Everything in our garden is rosy! I find this a typical statement from a member of the Establishment who is totally and completely out of touch with reality, moreover with the wants and needs of thalidomide victims.

May I remind you that every single law in this country that appertains to the regulation of taking and prescribing drugs is now in place as a direct result of the thalidomide tragedy? Having perused your website, it comes as no surprise to me that you are a medic yourself and therefore, Sir, I suggest that you seek to protect the ranks of your own kind who caused this massive debacle in the late 1950s to 60s and since then your old school tie network along with freemason involvement has meant that the old school tie brigade have all covered each other's backs in this war of attrition and you all long for the day that the last thalidomide victim leaves this Earth so you and your kind can sleep safely in your beds, not having to think of this huge tragedy bestowed on us by a government who failed in their duty of care and still fifty years on fail in their duty of care towards us.

Sir, let me advise you that if money were able to be passed down a hosepipe and placed on high pressure, you could not get enough of it, through either my front door or that of others like me, to compensate for the indignity, pain and suffering that we have endured over the last fifty years.

Quite frankly, I assume for your able-bodied self, nothing other than the comments that you made in the House because, as stated earlier in this correspondence, you are totally out of touch with reality. I find your comments ignorant at best and downright insulting at worst. I feel so strongly that I would suggest that, following your comments, you do the right thing and resign your post in the House of Lords, as your comments seek to hinder and not help our worthwhile campaign to right the wrongs that happened to us as individuals and moreover, to our mothers who were guaranteed that this was a safe drug to take with the blessings of their own GPs, which renders the government of the day vicariously liable for the tragedy.

Sir, I implore you to change your stance with regard to compensation to be paid directly from the government and further implore you to ensure that a substantial compensation package, financial and medical assistance, be put in place before the fiftieth anniversary on 1 October 2009.

I challenge you, if you concede to being out of touch with reality, to spend maybe a weekend or even a week with my good self and witness for yourself the problems that I face on a daily basis, and I Sir, am only two-limb deficient, thankfully with the use of my legs. The most severely disabled thalidomide victims, during days of depression, are not able to put on a coat and go for a walk.

I trust that this letter brings to your attention the stark realities of thalidomide and how it has severely blighted families, let alone individuals, for fifty years. The government of the day and the current government is Sir, a disgrace to allow this injustice to continue for one minute longer.

In closing, I note that you advised the House that an invitation to meet with officials from the Thalidomide Trust appears to have fallen on deaf ears. I believe, Sir, that to be a malicious falsehood and I am sure that should you take the time to write or telephone Dr Martin Johnson or the Honourable Mr Justice Wright (Sir Michael Wright), that they would down tools, change diaries etc. to meet with you or your staff.

I hope that my anger and disdain for your comments has come across loud and clear in this correspondence and I eagerly await your reply.

Yours Sincerely

Gary Skyner

Despite the publicity and the questions asked in Parliament nothing much seemed to be happening, until I got a phone call out of the blue from Nick Dobrik a few months later. He said,

'I'd like you to come to London. I need your help.'

I said, 'Why do you need my help? Why should I help you? You didn't help me.'

I still had a lot of bad feelings towards him because of the way he'd treated me in 2005.

He said, 'Let's put the past behind us and start clean,' so I arranged to meet him in the Hospital Club in Covent Garden, even though I was very suspicious as to what he wanted. John Smith came with me, and Dobrik knew I was angry with him. When we came into the club I think he was relieved that he wasn't going to be alone with me.

He must have thought that John's presence there would restrain me and he said,

'Come on, Gary, let's have some lunch,' and 'Hello, John, how are you?' and all that, as if we were best mates. All the way down I'd been threatening to fill him in and saying to John,

'Just let him say one wrong word and I'll snap.'

John Smith said to Dobrik, 'He's been threatening to kill you all the way down, and I've told him not to go down that road.'

Dobrik said, 'I must apologise. I was under pressure.' He was referring to the fiasco over my review at the Trust and I said,

'I don't give a fuck what you say. You fucking shat on me, and you know you did.' Anyway, things calmed down a bit and Daniel Foggo, a reporter from The *Sunday Times*, was there. He wanted to do a major article on the government and their involvement in the disaster. I was still pretty suspicious, and I said,

'So where do I come into it? What do you want from me?'

Dobrik said, 'We need someone to do something radical.'

I said, 'Oh, so fucking Soft-shite gets the pull.'

'We need someone to do something,' Dobrik said. 'You could do with losing a bit of weight. Why not go on hunger strike?'

I said, 'Why me? Why don't you do it?' But it was obvious. He didn't want to get his fingers dirty; didn't want to be in the *Sunday Ti*mes with everyone saying, 'Oh, he's a nutcase.'

I said, 'So you pick up the phone to Soft-shite and you think *I know he'll do it*, and, believe it or not, I fucking will do it.'

Dobrik started saying, 'Oh, wonderful,' but I wasn't letting him off that easily, and I said,

'But when I needed you in my hour of need you fucking deserted me.'

I came home and I spoke to Chris Johnson from the press. He was a good PR man and he said,

'On your own won't have much effect. How old's your

mum? You want to get a hotel to sponsor you to do the hunger strike so they can check you're not eating, you and your mum – and that'll make a good story.'

The Blenheim Lakeside Hotel in Sefton Park offered to do that, and even the Adelphi offered us a room. My mum was great, and Ricky Tomlinson came round to support us.

Mum and me looking hungry and unhappy on hunger strike.

When we'd been on hunger strike for a week GMTV turned up and the reporter asked my mum how old she was and she said,

'I'm seventy-two.'

The reporter asked, 'Do you take medication?'

She said, 'Yes, I do, for my blood pressure and for my heart.' So the reporter asked if it wasn't dangerous to take medication and not eat and my mum said,

'Oh, I just eat some Rice Krispies with it.'

I nearly died. I hadn't eaten for a week, and she's telling me she's been having a nice bowl of cereal. The worst thing was that it was live. There was nothing I could do about it. I thought *Fucking hell. She's a fucking nutcase. Get us off the telly now.*

After that my mum had to come off the hunger strike. It

was clear she couldn't continue because of her medication needs, but I think everyone appreciated her heroic effort. And, as expected, she certainly helped to raise the profile of the campaign. I carried on alone.

Labour was in power and Andy Burnham was the Health Secretary and Ricky Tomlinson and I were in the back kitchen doing a TV interview. Ricky went off on one, saying to the government,

'Come on. Step up to the plate. Fifty years on, and look at the state of these poor people,' and all that, and really went mad. The reporter from GMTV couldn't get a word in edgeways with Ricky because we were in Liverpool live and she was down in London in the studio and the producer was in our house, indicating to us to keep it going.

As soon as she'd finished the producer's mobile went off. It was a call to say someone from Andy Burnham's office had phoned the London studio and said to tell Mr Skyner and Mr Tomlinson to mind what they said while they were on live television, so Ricky shouted,

Ricky Tomlinson supporting Kevin Donellan and me in our campaign.

'Tell them if they've got anything to say to come to the studio. They're only round the corner.'

We were going down to meet Mike O'Brien, the health minister, and Ricky said to me,

'You've got my permission to go down there and tell him if he doesn't do the right thing that we'll bring a load of thalidomiders to camp on his fucking lawn and we'll stand against him in his own backyard. I'll put the money up and we'll call ourselves the "No Arms, No Legs, My Arse" party.'

I went down there and I grabbed Mike O'Brien in the House of Commons. He said,

'Get your hands off me.'

I said, 'Listen, mate. Fifty years of someone else wiping my arse and not one more fucking minute. You're going to sort this. I'm going to sort this out.' This was in October 2009 and he said,

'I have to go now. I'm going into a debate.'

We were there for this debate and we were searched and told if we said one thing we'd be thrown out. You remember that guy who put a custard pie in Rupert Murdoch's face in that enquiry over the phone hacking? How he got in there past the security I'll never know.

The Merseyside MPs were fantastic. Louise Ellman, Frank Field and others from the area... they were great. It wasn't really a Merseyside thing, but the MPs from the north-west really held out for us. Afterwards Mike O'Brien came straight to me and said,

'Look, I understand your frustration. I had the indignity of having to wipe my mum's backside while she was dying of cancer. I understand how she must have felt and how you feel, but please just relax and let us do the right thing.'

I said, 'I hope you do, because if you don't this is going to get bigger and bigger.'

So that was in the October, and I was still on hunger strike. It was a drastic step because my GP had strongly advised against it as I had a heart condition, but I was determined to go ahead. Somebody damaged me before birth and never said 'Sorry', and it was so wrong. I was prepared to die for it if necessary. I told the press during a Sky News interview,

'We need to highlight this to the public. If it means I stay without food indefinitely until I have to go in hospital, then so be it' (Sky News, 23 October 2009).

I began the hunger strike on 21 September and lost two and a half stones in thirty-two days. I came off hunger strike on my fiftieth birthday, 5 November, because we'd been told that the government had agreed to make an apology to the British thalidomiders and to discuss making a health grant to assist us in our daily living needs.

Celebrating my fiftieth with my mum.

The news broke just before Christmas that £20 million would be paid into a fund for our health needs over three years. But it wasn't until January 2010 that details were finalised and announced and the apology was officially issued on 14 January, with Mike O'Brien expressing the government's 'sincere regret and deep sympathy for the injury and suffering endured by all those affected' (Boseley, 2010).

I was on holiday with the lads in Florida at the time, and I was in bed when the phone started ringing. It was about five in the morning over there, and every British radio station was calling me to tell me the news of the funding. I said,

'Well, that's me sorted out. What about the others?'

I still wasn't happy. I said, 'It's a fucking insult, and it's fifty years too late.' Secretly I was made up, but fifty years is an awful long time to wait for both the cash and an apology.

I was also upset because I felt that Dobrik and the Trust had just used me to do the dirty work. When you look at the press reportage you would have thought I had nothing to do with it. As soon as that money was announced I never got a mention in the publicity. Yet it was me, Ricky and my mum doing what we did that brought the matter to public attention. Dobrik and Tweedy were lauded in the press for their roles in the negotiations. Ricky covered what we'd done in Ricky's Special Report, part of the BBC's *Inside Out* programme, but as far as the NAC went it was as if we never existed. So it goes. We just went home and put the balaclavas away till next time.

Following our government's decision the Welsh, the Scottish and the Northern Irish devolved administrations gave additional amounts to assist their own thalidomiders.

I should have been flushed with success, but in 2010 I found myself struggling to make sense of my life. The girls were growing up. Soon they would grow away and leave the nest. Shelagh and I seemed to stagger on, holding our marriage together as best we could. We had mutual needs, but were they enough to carry us through? More and more I felt unhappy and unfulfilled. Even though I had a good career and made a good living it wasn't enough. I was on a kind of plateau, with nothing new to achieve. I worked hard and earned money, which went on giving my family a good lifestyle, but what did it all mean? Was I really loved for myself? I found myself wondering where I was going and what lay in store for me. I'd just turned fifty. I had let myself go physically to the point where my weight was affecting my health, and I seemed to have lost direction. Was it just a midlife crisis, or the emergence of some long hidden despair that led me to do something really stupid that year?

The joker in the pack, but there were tears behind the laughter.

Chapter 13

Dark Days

It was February 2010. The year started badly for me. Work wasn't going so well. I'd been ousted from the thalidomide campaign, and my relationship with the Thalidomide Trust was at an all-time low. Clearly, I was the black sheep of the thalidomide family in their eyes. Shelagh and I were talking divorce – well, rowing about it, mostly – and when we weren't fighting we had little to say to each other.

When I was at home Shelagh would usually be playing games on her phone, and she paid me little attention. I felt embarrassed to ask her to do something for me like make a cup of tea, and it seemed that everything was a chore to her. I didn't know what had happened to the loving relationship we had once shared. When I looked in the mirror I saw a great fat unattractive bloke. I didn't see Gary the achiever, who was everybody's pal on stage. Even my daughters didn't want to be seen with me in public. That probably isn't true, but that's how I felt.

That year 9 February was one of those days when everything seemed to kick me in the teeth. Two gigs got cancelled, the girls were on my back about something at home and Shelagh joined in and we had a blazing row. By six o'clock, I'd had enough. I left the house in an absolute fury, slamming the doors, got in my car and drove.

I stopped at a garage and bought some packets of paracetamol. Without really thinking about it I found myself in Southport, parked near the beach. Southport was the home of Sylvia, the girl I'd had an affair with years earlier – the girl who would have meant something special to me if I hadn't already been married. I knew she was a paramedic working out of Southport and, as I sat in my car on the deserted front looking out at the empty beach, in the back of my mind was some vague idea that if I overdosed she would be the one who would come to my rescue. I'm a great believer in fate and things happening for a reason, but I wasn't thinking straight and probably getting fate mixed up with fantasy.

Anyway, I took twenty tablets and don't remember much after that except being sick. At some point someone started banging on the window. I think it was somebody looking for a drug deal, but I didn't have much to offer. I was pretty spaced out by then, and the next thing I knew there were blue flashing lights. The policeman opened the car door and asked if I was Gary Skyner.

I don't know why I did what I did. If I felt no one else loved me at least I knew that my mum did, and she would have been heartbroken if anything happened to me. It was a really selfish thing to do, but when you feel down like that you don't think rationally or consider other people. It seems odd for me to do something like that when I'm normally such an outgoing person, but it just goes to show how little you really know yourself and what is locked up inside you.

The police put me in their car and took me to A & E without waiting for an ambulance. It was about one thirty in the morning, and I don't remember anything then until I woke up in the psychiatric ward. I wondered what was going on when this bloke came up to my bed and started telling me about all these people he'd murdered, but a male nurse came and shooed him away. He reassured me that none of it was true, and then he brought me a cup of tea. He was really kind and said to me,

'You'll be all right now.' As he was leaving he told me, 'Your wife knows where you are, and she'll see you tomorrow.'

I was devastated. If I'd been in her shoes I'd have jumped straight in the car. It was only a few miles, but neither she nor the kids bothered to come. Maybe it wasn't quite the way I thought. Maybe she'd been told not to come in the middle of the night to avoid disturbing the ward. I don't know, but I felt it as just one more bit of evidence that nobody loved me or cared about me. I didn't find out till later that it was Hollie and Jessica who had alerted the police to look for me. Apparently I'd been in such a state when I left the house that they'd guessed I might do something stupid, so I suppose that shows that they did care about me after all.

I went home the next day and went back to muddling along in the marriage, but I still felt under pressure. I was still carrying on a running battle with the Thalidomide Trust over their refusal to accept that I'd been wrongly assessed from the very start in 1972. In 2011 I asked to see my file so I could find out exactly what had gone on, and they couldn't refuse because of the Freedom of Information Act.

I felt that they made it difficult for me, though, as Martin Johnson insisted that I had to go to their office in Huntingdon to look at it. However, that's exactly what I did. I think Johnson thought I would only be there for an hour or so but I spent eight hours going through the papers, and all that time he never let me out of his sight. That evening I took two of the office girls out for something to eat and they told me he never ever stayed in the office at lunchtimes, so obviously he'd felt I posed something of a threat.

Reading the correspondence that had gone backwards and forward about me as well as the numerous medical reports was enlightening, to say the least. It strengthened my determination to get a fair hearing for my case. I tried to put my family and work problems to one side, and plunged into the pursuit of justice from the Trust with renewed vigour. Our correspondence on the matter had already been ongoing for years, with me incurring substantial legal costs. If I'd known how much longer it would carry on I probably would have thought twice about it.

I wasn't the only thorn in the side of the Trust at this point. In fact I was probably only a minor irritation. In 2010 solicitors in Australia had mounted a campaign to identify possible thalidomide victims who had never been accepted as such. In the 1970s, when compensation was first mooted, a very stringent set of criteria was adopted for identifying a deformed child as thalidomide damaged. As well as limiting applicants to a certain timescale when the drug was available, and assessing evidence as to whether the mother had actually taken the drug, the physical damage caused by thalidomide was identified within a narrow band of injuries accepted as typical. These injuries were mostly confined to bilateral limb deformities of a fairly characteristic nature. These criteria remained the benchmark over decades yet, as the survivors grew and aged and medical knowledge of their condition expanded, it became clear that certain internal conditions – notably of the bowel and digestive system, together with hearing difficulties – could and should be included.

It was a worldwide problem, and one that solicitor Peter Gordon took by the horns in Australia when he began to gather rejected victims with a view to suing for compensation. His preparation of a case on behalf of Lyn Rowe, a fifty-three-year-old limbless woman, as a test case for a much larger group threatened to stir up a hornets' nest in many other countries. This case is so significant that the next chapter will be devoted to describing its development and outcome.

In the UK legal firms Leigh Day & Co. and Russell Jones

& Walker argued that new medical research could result in the number of recognised thalidomide victims being significantly increased (The *Sunday Times*, 26 June 2011, p. 12).

Now you'd think the Trust would be supportive, given that it is a charity dedicated to the aid of thalidomide victims. But this was not so. The Trust found itself in a cleft stick. Agreements had been reached with Diageo in the new covenant of 2005 that the company would not consider applications from new claimants, and that such claimants would in future need to apply through the Trust. Obviously the fund available for existing claimants might be seriously diluted, should the Trust be faced with a host of new claimants. When lawyers applied to it for the names of 350 applicants who had previously been rejected it stuck its head in the sand and refused to release them. Martin Johnson said there was no scientific evidence to support the claims (The *Sunday Times*, 26 June 2011). Despite all this a total of twenty-two new beneficiaries have been accepted by the Trust since taking on responsibility for new claimants.

When Grünenthal itself was approached the company's response was that it believed it had acted responsibly at all times in its development and marketing of the drug and would defend any claims (The *Sunday Times*, ibid.). Just how responsibly they had acted was clear from the evidence that was soon to be uncovered, but more of that later.

Maybe it was a response to the worrying proposal of a fresh batch of thalidomide claims that prompted Martin Johnson to take action (I don't know whether it was or not), but in November 2011 BBC News Magazine reported that he was working with Professor Ray Stokes from Glasgow University to investigate rumours that thalidomide had its origins in the Nazi prison camps of World War II. Meanwhile, on the other side of the world, the Australian lawyers were also digging into Grünenthal's past history. What they found made them determined to go gunning for the company.

Chapter 14

Changing the World

Sydney, Australia, 30 October 2010.

Lawyer Peter Gordon addresses a group of officially recognised Australian thalidomiders. The focus of his lecture is the absent thalidomiders, those who were never recognised as thalidomide damaged because their injuries failed to fit the narrow definitions of thalidomide damage made in the 1960s and 1970s. Included are those whose families never came forward because they thought their child's deformities were due to some fault in their genes or to some virus attacking the foetus in the womb. Gordon hopes to investigate such cases and to perhaps find enough evidence to make a claim for compensation for these lost victims, even at such a late stage in their lives.

In the audience sits Mary Henley-Collopy, a forty-nine-year-old thalidomider lacking both arms and legs. As she listens to Gordon's speech she remembers being at school with Lyn Rowe, a girl who had similar birth defects but who had always told Mary her injuries were due to a virus. Mary is still in touch with Lyn and her family, and when she returns home from the conference she rings Lyn's parents and urges them to contact Peter Gordon.

Despite having doubts, Wendy and Ian Rowe talk it over

with their daughter and decide to contact the lawyer. So begins a story that ends in a multi-million-dollar settlement for Lyn Rowe and creates implications for thalidomiders worldwide – recognised and unrecognised.

Lyn Rowe was born in 1962 lacking both arms and legs. Her parents already had two small daughters and coping with severe morning sickness at the start of the pregnancy took a toll on Wendy Rowe, which her doctor alleviated by giving her samples of a new drug Distaval. This drug had been given to him to try out by sales reps from DCBL, the Commonwealth distributors.

Following the shock of Lyn's birth the Rowes were told that their baby was unlikely to survive. They were advised to put her in a home and forget about her. It is a great tribute to them that they didn't do so. Lyn thrived under their care, and their dedication never wavered as they struggled to look after her for forty-nine years without any help or compensation. They had not applied for Lyn to be included in the group of Australian thalidomiders as, on questioning their doctor, they were told that Lyn's defects had been caused by a virus.

Now in their seventies, Wendy and Ian were finding it increasingly difficult to care for Lyn's growing health needs. A full-grown adult is considerably harder to lift and to care for than a small child, and the Rowes were fearfully aware that their own strength was waning as Lynn's physical needs increased with age. On top of that they had never had the money to buy a home that was truly suitable for wheelchair-bound Lyn, or to pay for the adaptations to their current home that might make life easier for them all.

In Australia in 2010 Diageo agreed to a voluntary top-up of $50 million (Australian dollars) to the country's existing thalidomiders. Although Michael Magazanik (*Silent Shock*, 2015, p. 45) sees this to some extent as a 'commendable act of corporate goodwill', it must be remembered that Diageo as a major worldwide drinks consortium is heavily reliant on public consumption of its products and is therefore forced to be sensitive to public opinion. As I have already shown in previous chapters, in my experience DCBL/Diageo only agrees to pay out when it feels threatened by adverse publicity.

In the wake of the publicity that followed the 2010 top-up Peter Gordon was hearing stories of unrecognised thalidomide victims, and began examining the criteria used in the 1970s to identify thalidomide-damaged children. He was soon convinced that many people had been wrongly excluded from claiming compensation, and he decided to take up their cases.

When he interviewed Lyn Rowe and her family he was so impressed by the urgency of their financial need that he had no hesitation in placing Lyn as the lead plaintiff in the planned litigation on behalf of the unrecognised Australian group. The claim was formally issued on 8 July 2011 and the defendants were named as Chemie Grünenthal, the original manufacturer of thalidomide, and the DCBL drinks company and its pharmaceutical subsidiary.

This was groundbreaking news. Chemie Grünenthal had never been successfully sued anywhere in the world for its role in the thalidomide disaster. The only proceedings against the company had been the criminal prosecution undertaken by the German government in 1968 which had eventually been dropped, allowing the firm to escape untouched. The only court case to be successfully pursued on behalf of a thalidomide victim was the case against US distributors Merrell Dow in 1971. This case resulted in a $2.75 million settlement for thalidomider Peggy McCarrick, and although this amount was later reduced, the final settlement still far exceeded anything else ever paid to a thalidomide victim before or since.

If Grünenthal was finally to be brought to book for the thalidomide disaster the eyes of the world would be on the case.

There would be worldwide implications for all thalidomiders who, like me, had nursed anger and resentment all their adult lives at the knowledge that the perpetrators of our difficulties had got off scot-free and showed no remorse or desire to make amends for what they had done. And, if there were over a hundred unrecognised thalidomide victims in Australia, how many more must there be worldwide? Enough to make Grünenthal tremble in its boots?

With this in mind, and conscious of the need to build a very strong case if Chemie Grünenthal was not to escape justice yet again, Peter Gordon's legal team began to dig through the history of thalidomide litigation and compensation deals. Lessons learnt from past failures as well as successes in many other countries were factored in to the growing mass of documentation. Included was material from Swedish cases and from the Federal Drug Agency records in the US as well as information from the UK compensation fight in the 1970s.

Some of the pitfalls that had caused earlier cases to fail had been resolved with time. Others still loomed. The right of the unborn child to sue is now recognised, thus excluding an escape route that Grünenthal had cruelly used in early cases. But there was still the statute of limitation which invalidated claims made after a certain number of years following the damage. However, this was a matter for the judge's discretion and, as damning evidence mounted, the team was optimistic that it would sway the judge to allow the claim.

Another problem was the gathering of written evidence and witness statements so long after the event. It is to the great credit of the lawyers that they were able to track down contemporary witnesses, members of the Rowe family, doctors and ex-DCBL salesmen who were still living and willing to testify.

But the most important find was a great mass of German documents which had formed part of the material deposited in connection with the criminal trial of Chemie Grünenthal's executives way back in 1968, material that had reposed untouched in a Düsseldorf archive ever since. The documents comprised letters and reports from Chemie Grünenthal detailing their handling of the sales of thalidomide, and of the escalating reports that the drug was having damaging effects. Once translated from the original German this material proved so damning that the lawyers felt it threw undeniable light on the company's guilt, which greatly enhanced Lyn Rowe's chances of success at law.

The new evidence was vitally important. Although both Chemie Grünenthal and Diageo were named as defendants, past experience showed that Grünenthal would be the hard nut to crack. It wasn't lost on the Australian lawyers that settlements we had achieved in the UK from Diageo were at least partly due to the pressure of public opinion and the demands of their own shareholders. Chemie Grünenthal, on the other hand, remained a family-based business that did not rely heavily on direct public buying power. The company had weathered the storm, continued to pursue a successful career and had steadfastly turned a deaf ear to pleas for it to formally accept responsibility and make proper amends. It had paid very little towards compensating its thousands of victims worldwide.

In Germany in 1970 the company made a very poor settlement. This was probably only done in order to allow the firm's executives to escape prosecution, as the company argued that the prosecution was preventing a settlement being made to the claimants. Another meagre settlement was made for a small group of Irish thalidomiders in the 1970s but after that there was nothing until Grünenthal made a €50 million contribution to the German government compensation fund in 2009. This may sound a lot, but divided between the German beneficiaries it amounted to around €18,000 each:

a paltry sum for a lifetime's disability. At least the German government made some provision for the victims. In many countries there had been no provision at all.

True to form, as soon as the Australian writ was issued, Grünenthal began delaying tactics and manoeuvres to extricate itself. The first ploy was to ask for the case to be heard in Germany rather than in Australia, which would have caused a whole host of logistic and language difficulties, particularly in view of Lyn Rowe's disabilities and healthcare needs. Fortunately this request was denied, and the trial date was set for October 2012. Both defendants then began to complain that the date was too soon and wouldn't allow them adequate time to prepare their defences, but Lyn's lawyers successfully argued that time was of the essence because of her urgent need. Apart from the request by the defendants for a time extension the question of whether the case would be brought at all, in view of the length of elapsed time between Lyn Rowe's birth and the date of claim, was still open and awaiting a judge's decision.

That question was never answered. On 18 July 2012 Diageo agreed to settle out of court, with Lyn Rowe accepting a multi-million dollar figure. The exact amount was not made public. Chemie Grünenthal paid nothing, getting off scot-free as usual. The company did not take part in the negotiations and, as it had all down the line, refused to accept any responsibility for birth defects or to show any compassion for its victims. Its behaviour made its subsequent 'apology' in September 2012, after fifty years of silence, appear a complete farce. It was a success story for Lyn Rowe and her family, who could now look forward to comfort for the remainder of her life, but it was galling to all us thalidomiders to see that once again Grünenthal had escaped justice despite the most appalling body of evidence.

The Lyn Rowe case caused – and still is causing – worldwide

ramifications that must be rocking Chemie Grünenthal's boat. At the press conference following the announcement of Lyn Rowe's settlement her father Ian told the world's press,

'You don't need arms and legs to change the world,' (Magazanik, 2015, p. 307) and I'm hopeful that this is proving true. Lyn's case was only a spearhead for all the other 107 Australian claimants who were represented by Peter Gordon.

Was it a coincidence that in September 2012 Grünenthal suddenly decided to issue an apology to thalidomide survivors and their families? From a cynical point of view it appeared as an attempt to pacify survivors around the world, who were now gathering together and pointing the finger at the company as the culprit that had totally escaped responsibility.

Although the apology offered 'sincere regrets' and 'deep sympathy for all those affected, their mothers and their families' (quoted in The *Sunday Times*, 1 September 2012, p. 3), the general tone was self-excusing and attempted to portray a caring company doing its best to make recompense. The well-worn excuse that the state of knowledge at the time could not have foretold the tragedy was trotted out once more and there was no mention of the past cover-ups, which would very soon make headline news in Magazanik's book.

Chemie Grünenthal also claimed to be making satisfactory recompense with the €50 million endowment and in the provision of hardship grants to individuals. The amount of €50 million divided between the thousands of thalidomiders worldwide (discounting all those who have died waiting) amounts to an insult of buttons.

Worst of all – and this is enough to make you laugh, if you didn't feel like crying or smashing something – was their excuse for totally ignoring our plight for over fifty years.

'We also apologise for the fact that we have not found our way to you from person to person for almost fifty years. Instead we have been silent, and we are very sorry for that.

We ask that you regard our long silence as a sign of the silent shock that your fate has caused us' (in The *Sunday Times*, op. cit.). This was such a farcical statement that Magazanik used the words 'silent shock' as the title for his damning book about Lyn Rowe's case.

The Grünenthal apology failed to serve its intended purpose and simply added fuel to the anger of thalidomiders around the world at the company's evasion of its responsibilities. As more and more groups of survivors began to communicate via social media they focused on making Grünenthal face up and pay up. Things were hotting up for Chemie Grünenthal, but at this point I had little involvement. The year 2012 was a catastrophic year for me, but even before then events in my personal life were preventing me from taking an interest in the wider picture.

Chapter 15

Losing My Rock

While all this was going on I was distracted because there was more heartbreak in store for me. In 2011 someone very special left my life. My Aunty Doreen was my dad's sister, but she and my mum remained the best of friends after he left. She disapproved of what my dad did, although she would never slag him off to us.

We had lots of happy holidays together and when her husband was dying I promised him I would look after her, and I did my best to keep that promise. She was always invited along on our family outings and nights out, and I made sure she was safely put in a taxi home at the end of each evening.

Even though she was in her eighties she was bright as a button, and such a switched-on lady. When she developed cancer at the age of eighty-three I was devastated. I went to see her in hospital. All the Skyner family members were tough, hard cases but she blew me away, saying,

'I know when I'm not going to be here any more.'

'Oh, don't talk soft,' I said and she said,

'No, the doctor's been this morning and I asked him how long I've got. I told him, "I want it straight," and he said, "OK. I reckon six months."' She was happy with that. She said now she could set her stall out.

At the end she was just skin and bone. I was at the foot of the bed and I was beside myself. She reached her hand out to me and said,

'You knew it was coming.'

She was a very tough woman and a really nice lady. I miss her so much.

My dad never came to the funeral, never even sent a message… his own sister. I didn't even get to speak to him when I phoned to break the news. Instead Marge just said she would pass the message on. She had no emotion, no word of sympathy.

Doreen's death was a big shock but worse, much worse, was to follow. In March 2012 my mum was going on a coach holiday to Torquay with her friend Edna, and I'd promised to give her some spending money. I was supposed to go and see her the day before she was leaving but it was a Sunday, I'd had a heavy night on the ale the night before and I had to do a gig at lunchtime. By the time I got back home I was knackered. I just wolfed my dinner down and got on the couch for a nap before the match started on TV. The next thing the phone went, and Jessica answered it. It was my mum and I shouted,

'Oh, OK. I know she's ringing for the money. Tell her I'll send you round with it.' I could hear my mum shouting, 'I'm not ringing for the money. I thought you'd want to come and see me before I went away. You never know… you might not see me again.'

I shouted back, 'Don't be a miserable cow. I'll send Jess down with the papers and the money.'

Jess came and said she really had wanted to see me, so I phoned her back and she started laying it on, saying,

'Oh, I just thought you might be able to spare the time to come and see your mother,' and all that, but I didn't go.

She went with her mate Edna, and she rang our Karen a few times and said she was having a good time.

On the Thursday the office suddenly went stony cold. The office is in my house, and my PA Steven wasn't around. I sat outside where it was a bit warmer, because I couldn't reach the thermostat to switch the heating on. Shelagh came back from shopping and I came indoors and asked her to put the heating on. I got on the couch and she was making a cup of tea when the phone went. Shelagh answered, and I could tell there was something wrong. I kept saying,

'What's up?' but she wouldn't answer me. She just kept talking to Steven. I'm trying to listen in and I'm saying, 'What the fuck's up?'

She put the phone down and said, 'That was Steven. It's your mum. Someone's been in touch, someone from the group on the coach.'

I said, 'Why? What's up with my mum?' and she said,

'They don't know where Edna is.'

I thought they'd gone missing or something. Then she said, 'Your mother's had a heart attack.'

I'm on my feet then, ready to get my coat on and to drive to Torquay. Shelagh said,

'She had a heart attack at one o'clock and she died.'

I didn't know what to say. I kept saying, 'Are you sure?'

What had happened was this. As soon as they'd pronounced her dead at the hospital Edna had packed all her stuff and all my mum's stuff and got a taxi all the way back to Liverpool without telling anybody. In the confusion no one was sure which of them had had the heart attack. It's a terrible thing to say but I had a slight glimmer of hope that it was Edna and not my mum because Devon and Cornwall Police told us it was one of the two. But they weren't sure which one it was until they found Edna, as they looked quite similar.

I rang the hotel and spoke to the manager, who said he couldn't talk to me about it. All the rest of the group of women with my mum had gone on a trip that day, so until they came back nobody knew what had happened or could identify her.

Eventually, at about nine thirty, the police came and told me it was definitely her. Edna told me later they'd had a really good time at the hotel. The night before my mum had fallen off the loo in the bedroom and they'd been laughing their heads off about it. They got up to make a cup of tea, and the steam from the kettle had set the smoke alarm off. Two big security guards had come to investigate and my mum had said,

'Now we know how to get some men in our room.'

Mum and Edna, the Cheeky Girls.

The next morning they'd had a full breakfast and decided to miss the trip and spend the day relaxing at the hotel. They sat in the lounge reading the papers and having coffee and cake. They planned to go out later, sit on the front and have a late chippy lunch. But while Edna was ringing for a taxi my mum collapsed, and despite the efforts of the staff to give CPR and the prompt arrival of an ambulance they couldn't do anything for her. She was pronounced dead at 1.30 p.m. at the hospital.

I was booked to do a motivational talk the next day and Steven said he would cancel it but I said,

'No. There're 300 people involved. I can't let them down.'

I went and I thought I was OK till I remembered that in

the video I show as part of the talk my mum is filmed making a cup of tea. That was it. I had to go behind the curtain for a little weep. It was devastating. The only woman who ever really loved me was gone just like that. But at least I could cling to the belief that she didn't suffer.

It was a good funeral, if there can be such a thing. There were lots of friends and relations there. I never heard anyone give her a bad word, and she was like a Florence Nightingale. She worked in Mossley Hill Hospital, which is over the road from where I'm living now. Again, my dad didn't show. He didn't even respond to the news or send a card or anything.

I sank into a low mood. Mum's death dealt me a terrible blow, and towards the end of the year I felt suicidal again and tried to take my life. This time Shelagh and I had been out together and we'd started rowing in a wine bar near our house. I told her to go home – just to put a stop to it, really. She went but she rang John Smith and he came down and tried to get me to go home, but I wouldn't. I persuaded him that I was all right, and I ended up down town in McCartney's bar in Hanover Street.

I don't know how many whiskies I drank. Then I flagged a taxi and told the driver to stop at a garage on the Dock Road, where I got a pasty and forty paracetamol tablets. I asked the cabbie to drop me off on Otterspool Prom and he was suspicious, as there was no reason to be there late at night. I said I was going to Ricky Tomlinson's home and he didn't want people to know where he lived so I would walk from the prom. But I had no intention of going there. The driver dropped me off outside the Otterspool pub which, by then, was shut for the night, and I sat outside on a bench and ate half the pasty and took one box of tablets. I lay down on one of the wooden tables. It was freezing but I just lay there, wanting to die.

The next thing I remember was some headlights flooding the car park, and it was a police car. I don't know how it got there. The police called an ambulance and I got rushed to the Royal Hospital. After this I was put on antidepressant medication but it didn't help much.

Although Shelagh and I stayed together it was still a rocky relationship. I always felt at a disadvantage in an argument as I was dependent on her for care, so I daren't upset the apple cart. I put most of my energies into earning more money. Maybe I felt I had to buy the family's affection, but that has always been my way. I feel I have to repay any favour.

In May 2013 I planned once again to end it all. I was on my way to a booking to speak at a sporting dinner. I felt really down and stopped by a lake. I was thinking about suicide but I dozed off, and only woke up when someone from the venue phoned to see where I was. I went there and did the show. I went down really well but I still didn't feel any better. I stopped on the way back and thought how hopeless my life seemed to be. The only way out seemed to stare me in the face.

Earlier in the day I'd written a poem about suicide and posted it on Facebook. I have a huge group of Facebook friends and some of them were alarmed by what I'd written and alerted Shelagh, who then rang the police. Once again I was found, and disaster was averted.

All this time I'd been carrying on a bitter battle with the Thalidomide Trust for what I considered to be my right to have my allocation reassessed all the way back to 1972 (instead of the arbitrary cut-off point of 1992 that they insisted on). During my visit to Huntingdon I found correspondence on my file dating back to 1992 which expressed concern about my psychological state and recommended some form of intervention. This had never been acted on, so I decided to take the matter up. I paid for psychological and psychiatric reports to be prepared to see if earlier intervention might have been beneficial and to see if thalidomide damage was responsible for my mental health problems.

Apart from the battle with the Trust I was alarmed at my low moods and the deterioration in my family relationships… and without my mum, who'd always been my rock, the future seemed increasingly scary.

Both reports found that I had suffered for a long time from mental health problems, probably since 1971 or earlier – and certainly since 1991, when I was reassessed by the Trust's medical officer. The reports concluded that because of my circumstances I would probably always suffer chronic mental health issues, but that earlier intervention could have helped.

Various treatments and therapies were recommended but both professionals picked up on the deterioration in my mental state since I no longer had the stability of the relationship with my mum, and how the problems with Shelagh and my daughters had also increased in this period. If the family was to stay together the reports recommended engaging a personal carer for me. This would take some of the stress off Shelagh and create a more equal relationship between us, where I would be less reliant on her.

It was food for thought. We began to engage paid carers, but most of them were hopeless. They wouldn't dry me properly and stuff like that, and I wasn't the type to say,

'Oh, you haven't done that right,' so I'd try to do it myself, and would end up getting sores and stuff because I couldn't manage it.

Shelagh didn't like me having carers as they were usually women, and she didn't like that. So I was looking for male carers, and they were nearly always people who were just doing that job because they couldn't get anything else. They were not really caring, not really good at what they did. Fortunately my old friend John Smith often stepped into the breach, and I am indebted to him for his help and care to this day. I was still badly overweight and drinking heavily, and I was advised to cut down severely on alcohol and unhealthy food. That's hard to do when you earn your living in clubs and at dinner events, but I have gradually managed to cut down a lot.

Armed with these new reports, I renewed negotiations with the Trust. But by now Martin Johnson and I were pretty much at loggerheads. In 2013 he retired quite suddenly, and I was left wondering what the new director would be like. Easier to deal with, or more difficult?

The new director, Deborah Jack, soon took up the post in 2014, and I hoped a fresh relationship would be beneficial for me. The chair had also changed in 2012. Judge Michael Wright was replaced by Sir Robert Nelson.

Motivational speech in Hundith Hill, Cumbria, 2013: still badly overweight.

One of the reports I had commissioned linked my problems to thalidomide. The other wouldn't state categorically that they were due to thalidomide and it implied that they could have been caused by other life events, so we couldn't really use it in court. My lawyers said if we had to go to court and the Trust fought the case I could end up losing a lot of money. We had hoped that if the reports had made a cast-iron case then the Trust would have capitulated and been willing to talk. The case wasn't really strong enough, and I could see it wasn't worth pursuing it further. Sometimes you just have to give up and call it a day. Nothing much changed for me in 2014. I still felt low, and I still had all the same problems.

On top of that I couldn't get over losing my mum. I

just missed her so much every day. One day I found myself up in Cumbria near Ambleside. It was the same old story: paracetamol tablets in the car; misery in my heart. I sat there all day, staring at the lake, thinking, *There's nothing left*, but before I got round to taking the tablets a police car pulled into the car park. A policewoman got out and said,

'Are you Gary? Have you had enough?'

I said, 'Yes, I've had enough. Do me a favour, babe. Back your van up and let me go.'

She said, 'You're not going anywhere,' and I ended up in the hospital in Kendal where they sectioned me under the Mental Health Act and locked me up. Two psychiatrists had to come out to assess me. It was about two in the morning. In the morning John turned up with Shelagh and they let me go, provided I was released into their custody and saw my GP the next day.

I told the doctor that the whole pack of cards seemed to be tumbling down, and he told me that I needed to slow down and concentrate on looking after myself instead of running around trying to change things all the time.

Not long after that I went to London to visit an old friend of mine who was in hospital with cancer. He'd had a growth removed and was having chemotherapy. I saw how much he wanted to live, and it made me feel ashamed. He would have gladly swapped places with me, and I'd been sitting there swallowing tablets and acting like a dickhead. I realised how stupid I had been and swore to myself, *never again*.

I still have the odd blip, but now I know I'm over the worst. I won't do that again.

In July 2014 the lawyers Leigh Day & Co. succeeded in getting a rejected applicant recognised as being thalidomide damaged. Fifty-three-year-old David Tickell from Chichester had formerly been refused recognition by the Trust but, following the presentation of witness and medical evidence by the law firm, he was finally admitted to the hallowed ranks after many years of rejection.

This set another precedent. Things were beginning to look grim for governments and distributors of the drug around the world, and also for Chemie Grünenthal itself.

The Australian lawyers followed up the success of Lyn Rowe's litigation with further cases. Again a painstaking process of collecting evidence was needed, but in 2013 Diageo also settled these claims at a total lump sum of $89 million (Australian dollars). Once more Chemie Grünenthal contributed nothing. The world was watching and thalidomiders everywhere were disgusted by Grünenthal's attitude, especially after their worthless so-called 'apology' in 2012.

In 2013 the Spanish organisation Avite had taken Chemie Grünenthal to court directly, and won. In the past the Spanish government had denied that thalidomide was ever used in Spain, yet despite being withdrawn throughout the rest of the world, stocks continued to be used there throughout the 1970s and babies with typical thalidomide deformities were born as late as the early 1980s (Scott, 2015). Many families did not even know about thalidomide, let alone identify it as being responsible for their child's birth defects, so for many it was not until the late 1990s that they realised what had happened to them. Avite's victory gave these families only a small amount of compensation, but it seemed to set a precedent for future cases elsewhere. Unfortunately the decision was overturned on appeal on the grounds that the claims had come too late. At times it certainly seems that Chemie Grünenthal has the luck of the devil.

And so the company that created us thalidomiders persisted in clinging to its rock of denial. How long could it go on resisting the tide of condemnation that surrounded it? The original perpetrators of the nightmare are long gone, leaving us – their legacy – behind to haunt the firm's current owners and executives.

Would it be so hard for them to own up to what the company did now, after the passage of time? Would it be so hard to finally do the right thing, and to do their best to mitigate the damage and make life comfortable for the survivors? The wealthy Wirtz family still owns the company, and the firm's assets are healthy. Apart from the €50 million in 2009 they made no contribution, even in their own country. Chemie Grünenthal made no input, despite the German government having to raise the pensions of thalidomiders substantially in 2013.

With each passing year, as Grünenthal maintains its aloof stance and refuses to recognise its responsibilities, the number of thalidomide survivors dwindles as their health deteriorates with increasing age. Most of us bear a deep rage towards Chemie Grünenthal – not so much for what it has done to us, but for the way it has refused to acknowledge us and make amends for what they made us.

In the book *Silent Shock* (Magazanik, 2015) there is a photograph of Monika Eisenberg, a German thalidomider. She is standing outside the Chemie Grünenthal plant in Aachen beside a huge banner proclaiming:

Made in Grünenthal – Successful in the world.

Monika argues in the book that thalidomiders were made by Grünenthal and some of us have been successful in the world, so perhaps the company's boast is true. But many of its victims died in the womb or a few days after birth. Others have lived out their lives in institutions and care homes. Many of us have struggled financially, our families and relationships broken by the burdens of care and worry.

It's little wonder that Chemie Grünenthal's farcical

'apology' in 2012 served only to enrage many of us further. It might have been more credible if they had at least backed it up with a promise to do something to ease the problems of declining health which loom for the remaining thalidomiders, but it seems the company is happy to continue to play out a waiting game until we are all dead and no longer able to pose any threat.

The UK government had agreed to extend the health grants given in 2009 for another ten years but it wasn't enough, and it wasn't the government which had the prime responsibility. In August 2014 Leigh Day & Co., following in Peter Gordon's footsteps, published their intention to sue Grünenthal on behalf of a group of unrecognised British thalidomiders. And in November 2014 the Thalidomide Trust reported on the finding of incriminating correspondence and documents relating to Chemie Grünenthal's production and marketing of thalidomide in the 1950s, papers that had been suppressed at the time of their aborted trial in Germany.

It seemed that the net might be closing in on Chemie Grünenthal but I knew what a slippery fish the company was, and all this negotiation between institutions and governments was slow... so slow. I'd bottled up my anger ever since the 1990s when I became aware of Chemie Grünenthal's treachery. I'd been able to dissipate some of my rage through the campaigns against Diageo but, following these latest events – and after learning that Grünenthal had yet again managed to slither out of their responsibilities – in the winter of 2014–5 I decided to have a go at them myself.

Chapter 16

Still Smouldering After All These Years

In January 2015 I went on holiday to Cuba with friends. It was a good trip, but at the same time I was laying plans to shame Chemie Grünenthal in the public arena yet again. I hoped I could open up a dialogue that might result in useful negotiations.

On my return I contacted Grünenthal's British office and informed them I would be going on hunger strike until the company agreed to come to the table for serious talks. In February, having had no positive response, I began the strike under medical supervision. I took only fluids and vitamin supplements, and I informed as many media sources as possible.

Unlike on previous occasions I did not get the support I'd hoped for from other thalidomiders. I've always published whatever I'm doing on Facebook, and my latest venture set off a furore of debate. Some people supported me wholeheartedly. Others, including many thalidomiders, were outspokenly critical, saying that my actions would interfere with the negotiations being conducted by the NAC.

Never one to mince words, I gave back as good as I got. There were some heated exchanges, but I was determined to carry on.

I stayed on hunger strike for thirty-two days, but as

the weeks went by there was only silence from Chemie Grünenthal. In that period I lost two and a half stones.

I was still fulfilling all my comedy and motivational speaking engagements, but it was obvious that I couldn't continue without eating indefinitely – although, in my mind, I was convinced I would go to the bitter end.

I decided that something drastic needed to be done, something that would stimulate media attention. And so I chose to picket the Chemie Grünenthal British offices, which are situated in High Wycombe. I notified the company of my intention and the proposed date, and this eventually brought some response. The firm's executives informed me that there was little point in my venture and that they could not cater for me, as their building was unsuitable and had no disabled facilities.

Looking and feeling grim towards the end of the hunger strike in 2015.

It was obviously a ploy to put me off, and I told them as much. They then offered to book a hotel room for me but I had no intention of accepting this, and had in fact already booked alternative accommodation for myself and the team who would be coming with me.

I had hoped that other thalidomiders would support

me and turn up on the day, but for the most part that didn't happen. Only a small group of us was there to challenge this heartless company, a fact that must have given those inside the building some satisfaction.

We arrived very early in the morning and took up position. I was dressed only in an outsize nappy and was armed with a giant baby's feeding bottle. Knocking and buzzing at the entrance door brought no response, but after a short time a security van showed up. The driver left after we explained what was going on and a bit later the police showed up, but there was no sign of the Grünenthal executives we had come to see. The door remained firmly closed all the time we were there. Were they so afraid of Gary, the terrible wild card? And there I was like a big, (h)armless baby.

Me in High Wycombe

The worst insult of the day was the ridiculous portable disabled toilet they had placed in the car park for my use so they wouldn't have to let me in the building. We had a laugh about it, but really I was so angry that I had to be restrained from putting a match to it.

On my return home I received an invitation to meet with representatives from Grünenthal's German headquarters, so I came off hunger strike and prepared for the meeting. I was hopeful that something sensible might come from it, but I didn't hold my breath. Weeks went by as Chemie Grünenthal dragged its heels, procrastinating over the date, the venue and who would be allowed to attend.

Disabled toilet that was placed in the car park of the Grünenthal site

Eventually the meeting was set for John Lennon Airport in February 2015. Two German executives arrived, but right from the start it was clear that the whole thing was just a farce. From the choice of venue it was obvious that they just planned to fly in, throw us a sop and fly out again. From the beginning I could see that they were bringing nothing new to the table.

I could see the cold determination in their eyes as they kept repeating the same mantras:

'We will help you with your health needs. We will fix your teeth. We will give you special beds,' and so on and so on. It was the same old stuff they had promised thalidomiders in 2012, delivered as if they were doing me a big favour. After ten minutes I got up and stormed out. I knew if I stayed I would end up planting one of them. It wasn't charity I wanted, and they knew it.

After that I was asked by the Trust not to intervene further. I was upset, but did as I was asked. In any case my life at home had turned upside down, and I had little time for anything beyond sorting out my personal circumstances.

Things hadn't been good between Shelagh and me for a long time. I was away from home a lot, and Shelagh was always accusing me of having affairs with other women. Obviously the clubs and dinner venues I worked at did offer opportunities, but for the most part her suspicions were completely unfounded. It got so bad that I felt estranged in my own home. The girls took her side in everything, and we seemed to be on the point of splitting up.

With the help of an advance on my annual allowance from the Trust I rented a small flat not far from my house. I was using it as an office but I was thinking about getting away and using it as a bolthole, so we could both have some breathing space. I hadn't really done much with it when Katrina, my mate John's sister, offered to help me pick out some furniture for it. I was happy for her to do that because I'm hopeless. I knew she would do it in good taste, whereas if it was left to me everything would be red and decorated with Liverpool scarves and posters.

I was apprehensive about leaving home. I didn't know how I would manage, but at times it seems that someone up there is looking out for me. Just at the time when I really needed a good carer a young man, Shabi, was recommended to me by another carer whom I had asked for help. He has been an absolute godsend to me, and I don't know how I would ever cope without him now. John Smith, Katrina and Gail Edwards also came together to help me with household matters. It seemed to all happen as if it was meant.

I thought the attention would soon wind down, but everyone has been fantastic. I've been encouraged to look after myself better, eat healthily and do more exercise. I've kept the weight off that I lost on hunger strike, and continue to reduce my weight on a supervised diet. I feel better than I have in a long time, and I'm so grateful to everyone who has rallied round to help me. Without that support I would have felt obliged to try and return home but I would have felt beaten, and I know it wouldn't have worked out.

Of course there are major disadvantages and heartbreak involved in a divorce. I feel that I have lost my daughters to some extent, as I don't see as much of them now. That's heartbreaking, but I can only hope that time will mend our relationship. I miss my beloved boxer dogs too. I've hardly seen them since the divorce proceedings started.

At times I do feel lonely and miss the family side of life, but I was always away from home a lot and now I'm free to concentrate on developing my work. At least the girls are grown up now and able to make their own way in the world. Shelagh too will be free to pursue a life of her own and find her identity, something she says she could never do when she was with me.

I feel I am at a crossroads, with old relationships breaking up and the prospect of new and unknown things ahead. Of course I have regrets – thirty years of marriage and family life down the drain – but I still have two lovely girls to show for it.

Hollie and Jessica

My sister Karen and I have also always had a stormy relationship but now I feel we are starting to put aside our differences, so I hope we can be friends.

Best man at Karen's wedding.

It's the same with the Trust. Since 2014 things have been much better, and I feel our relationship is more comfortable. Without the financial help I received this year I wouldn't have been able to get the flat and make the changes that have helped me physically and psychologically. For that reason I decided not to pursue the claim for reassessment, and I also agreed not to intervene further in compensation negotiations.

The NAC is taking such negotiations to a new level. Meetings are being organised in Brussels with the European Health Commission, and they are also lobbying the German government. In my personal opinion they persist in running on a hamster wheel while Chemie Grünenthal wait for us all to die off, whereas I just want to go in and rip the cage apart. But I've agreed to withdraw. I'm content that in the past I've played my part, and I'll be ready to do so again in the future if and when it becomes necessary. It's a bit like a jigsaw, where every piece is essential to complete the picture.

So... to the future. Over the last few years I've seemed to

be at a stalemate and, for a go-getter like me, that feeling has resulted in the dark days that have dogged me. But 2015 has brought change and a fresh wind, so to speak.

I want to continue and expand my role as a motivational speaker. There are so many people who feel disadvantaged in some way, and I feel that my story has resonance for a wide audience. I'm a larger-than-life example of how to overcome the shit life can throw at you and turn it into a life of valuable experience.

You might think that my suicide attempts belie that statement but I'm brave enough to admit my weaknesses, and the fact that I have come through that dark patch and turned my life around yet again only shows that you can change your life for the better. Secretly though, I often think that divine intervention had something to do with it. The way things have turned out for the best and the way certain people who have helped me through difficult times turn up just when needed… I can't help thinking my mum is driving the bus, watching over me somewhere up there.

I was booked to speak at a residential event recently and there was a chaplain present and, over the couple of days I was there, I told him some of my story. On the second day he said to me,

'I've got a message for you,' and I said,

'Oh, who from?' thinking it was someone from the office. He said, 'No, it's from God.'

I said, 'Oh, so the gaffer's been in touch?'

He said, 'Yes. You know you said in your speech that you were a mistake? Well, you're not a mistake. God set you to carry this burden and to spread the word, and that's what he meant you to do. That's your mission. Spread the word about how evil can be overcome.'

So I think about mission and purpose, where I've come from and where I'm going and how have the years changed me. For most of my adult life I saw my purpose as being a provider, earning money to support my lifestyle and to give my wife and kids everything they wanted. Now I no longer need to fulfil that role, although I would never see them suffer hardship.

One of my many motivational speaking events.

And my mission in life has always been to achieve. That is one in the eye for my dad, and his poor opinion of my capabilities. That too has gone. I don't want to fly a jumbo jet or climb Mount Everest. I no longer feel I have to prove myself. I've been through struggles and despair, but also triumphs and great joys. I will never be able to sit back and do nothing – a Scorpio is never content – but I'm happy with who I am. My aspirations now are to be happy, healthy and to try to do the right thing. I'm always mischievous, though, and there is one practical stunt I would love to pull.

When we thalidomiders were born we were often called monster babies because of the teratogenic nature of our deformities. I am an excellent swimmer and I would dearly love to grease up and swim the icy waters of Loch Ness, proving once and for all that Nessie really does exist. It would be a great publicity stunt, but it's just one of the plans I keep in the back of my mind for when the day comes that such publicity may be needed.

I'd like to think I've done some good in society and I'd like to be remembered for that, even though I am labelled a loose cannon. Throughout life I've often wondered why I'm here and why I was born the way I was. Only now, with the hindsight of years, can I see a pattern emerging. Through the turmoil of life, the cruelty of disability, the ups and downs of struggling to survive, to make a good life… Through the joys of love and marriage and children, the pain and despair of losing those you love the most… Something shines through.

That chaplain touched on it, but it isn't just me. We, the surviving thalidomiders, are a living testament to the consequences of carelessness and greed. While we exist we shame the company that made us, and signpost its continued arrogance, heartlessness and neglect of duty.

We are also a reminder that what is on the outside is no pointer to what is on the inside, and that we all have a part to play in society. Because of us new laws were made governing the production and marketing of drugs, in an effort to avoid another tragedy on this scale. Despite this, thalidomide babies are still being born in countries like Brazil – where the drug is used to treat symptoms of leprosy – but numbers worldwide are minimised by the stringent safety procedures now in place. The drug is tolerated because of its overwhelming beneficial effects in the treatment of autoimmune conditions, while new and safer forms of it are being developed. More recently it is proving efficacious in the treatment of some cancers, so it seems that even thalidomide has a valuable part to play in the world.

Because of us the details of a great tragedy are recorded for posterity. We are a warning to future generations, a reminder that human health is more important than the pride of scientists or the profit motive of commerce.

Also, as a body, we are an inspiration to others. The majority of us, despite our disabilities, have achieved careers, marriage and children, happy and fulfilling lives, which shows just what determination can achieve. To all those who are downtrodden, broken in one way or another – or in seemingly impossible situations or lacking self-confidence – we demonstrate hope. If we can make a go of life, who can't?

And we are determined in our continued fight for our rights – and the rights to be financially independent, with respect to our care needs, for the remainder of our lives. No longer isolated in individual countries, thalidomide groups are joining forces to make those responsible for our condition stand up and do the right thing. And this fight will go on while we still have breath.

People approach this fight in different ways. I may feel some approaches are wrong and so I've agreed to step back for now, but my greatest desire is to see Chemie Grünenthal brought to justice in my lifetime.

Remember, remember, the fifth of November. I was born on Guy Fawkes Night, and I'm still smouldering.

Chapter 17

The Special Ones

FRANCES SKYNER

This lady does not just come top of the list of special ones, but was the kindest, loveliest human being I have ever met. She was everything to me throughout my life. I miss her more every day that passes.

SHELAGH SKYNER, née ROONEY

Now my ex-wife, but Shelagh arrived on the Gary scene when in truth I wasn't looking for a relationship.

She shared twenty-nine years of my life, if you include the year we courted. She would probably tell a totally different story to mine, but our relationship was destined to fail in the long run because we differed in so many ways. From tastes in furniture to clothes, music and food, etc., we were like chalk and cheese.

We must have loved each other in our own way, but many a day seemed like a battle and in later days she seldom wore a smile. She clearly had grown tired of me, for whatever reason. Don't get me wrong: with severe disability comes frustration and anger and, as they always say, you hurt the one you love.

JOHN VERNON SMITH

I always refer to John as my stand-in dad. By the time this book is published I will have known him for a total of fifty years. I met him through my footballing friendship with his son John Smith, and you have already read the story of that in this book. As well as encouraging me and helping me financially to join a football team in my youth, he was a boilermaker with his own welding firm and he trained me as a welder, despite my disabilities.

Over the years we have shared life's ups and downs, with many emotional experiences. We have also had many great holidays together, travelling all over the world to places like Argentina, Florida, South Africa, New York and the Bahamas, as well as the usual European resorts. I have been his lawyer, his employee, his travel companion and his guide. He has been my employer, my saviour (often from myself!) my confidant, my bodyguard and carer, but most of all I see him as my dad. He will be seventy-five next birthday but doesn't look a day over sixty. Long may he continue.

JIMMY COULTHARD

Jimbo, as I affectionately call him, is your original caveman. He grew up in the Liverpool outskirts in Speke. He has a reputation for being a tough cookie – and he is – but we have enjoyed a thirty-five-year friendship that has seen many holidays, many late-night drinking sessions and many fallings-out.

We never fall out for long, but we are not afraid of telling each other exactly how it is. We have played football together, and I have been his mate, coach, manager, and – he would probably say – the bane of his life.

KENNY HARVEY (deceased)

Kenny and I met through a kissogram. Shelagh arranged a sexy nurse on my birthday to come to Maranto's in Lark Lane. Kenny was the video man who arrived with the stripper and the top hat and tails man.

I arranged to buy the video of the event and of course swapped telephone numbers with Kenny. He became a dear family friend who travelled abroad with me as not just my friend, but as my carer and mentor. Kenny is sadly missed.

JOHNNY HOPKINS

When I started work at Unicorn Road Day Centre in Croxteth Johnny was a great friend to George Devlin.

Johnny was a senior shop steward at Yorkshire Imperial Metals on the East Lancashire Road. He was a 'never say die' type of shop steward. His bosses loathed him because he was like a dog with a bone. He never let go when he knew there was injustice in a case.

Because I had a dual career working for the city council and as an entertainer the green-eyed monster often reared its ugly head and I was singled out for discrimination. I always brought in Johnny. I learnt a lot from him in my days of legal study, especially the skill of tough advocacy.

VINNY HARVEY

Vinny started life as a journalist with the *Liverpool Echo* and worked alongside Anne Robinson, a big hitter in the journalism world at that time.

Vinny is a big Beatles fan, and plays a mean guitar himself. He became my carer and my driver and my great friend and, like me, had a devotion to fine whisky. We would often join each other in overindulgence.

Vinny was blessed, as I was, with two lovely daughters: Caroline and Louise. Caroline became a paramedic, and because I am a hypochondriac I had her regularly demented when I enquired if this was wind pain or a cardiac arrest. The Harveys, who include mother Vera, are a lovely family and dear friends.

IAN WEBB

Ian lived in Aspen Grove the road where I grew up, and his father George Webb was the senior police dog handler in Liverpool in the 1970s.

The Webbs lived in one of the six police houses at the bottom of Aspen Grove. Ian's mum was the senior dinner lady at Tiber Street infant school. Ethel Webb was probably the sole reason I was a chubby little boy, because she always made sure I had loads to eat at dinnertime and brought me seconds constantly.

Both George and Ethel have passed now. Ian was one of those people who have been with me throughout my life, until we had two massive fallings-out. The first one happened when he interfered in my marriage. He had become my brother-in-law, as he married my wife's sister, Maria Rooney, but I didn't think that entitled him to get involved.

We had only just managed to start speaking to each other again when his wife Maria left him. Because I spoke with her new partner Ian saw that as disloyalty on my part, but I couldn't refuse to welcome my wife's sister and her new partner into my home. The fact that my wife and I were constantly on a knife-edge meant that I wanted to avoid further family pressures from external sources.

It seems that Ian Webb and I have fallen out irreconcilably, even though I too now have suffered the same divorce scenario.

KATRINA EDWARDS

I've been friends with Katrina Edwards's family for many years, so we have known each other since way back. During the upheaval of the divorce Katrina was one of those who stepped in to help me move into the flat, and she also took over some aspects of my personal care. Since then she has come to mean so much more than a carer and friend, and I hope our relationship will continue to deepen and gain strength. Thank you, Katrina, for being there when I most needed someone.

I call these people the 'Special Ones' because they have gone beyond friendship, and have not balked at supporting me and giving me physical care, which is a difficult thing for a man to have to admit. Without these people life would have been far more challenging on many occasions.

I WILL NEVER BE ABLE TO THANK THEM ENOUGH.

References

Books

Brynner, R. & Stephens, T., *Dark Remedy*, (2001), New York, USA, Basic Books/Perseus Books.

Gath, L., *Don't Tell Me I Can't*, (2011), Ireland, Book Republic/ Maverick House.

McBride, W., *Killing the Messenger*, (1994), Cremorne, NSW, Australia, Eldorado Publishing Ltd.

Magazanik, M., *Silent Shock*, (2015), Melbourne, Australia, Text Publishing.

Medus, L. & Swain, G., *No Hands to Hold and No Legs to Dance On*, (2009), Mountain Ash, Wales, Accent Press.

Sampson, D. & Skyner, G., *Turned a Tear Into a Triumph*, (2006), Liverpool, UK, Gary Skyner.

The *Sunday Times* Insight Team, *Suffer the Children*, (1979), London, UK, Andre Deutsch Ltd.

Newspaper and Magazine Articles

Boseley, S. 'Thalidomide victims launch battle for more compensation'.

The *Guardian* (4 April 2008).

Boseley, S. '50 years on, an apology to thalidomide scandal survivors'.

The *Guardian* (14 January 2010).

Evans, H. 'Thalidomide: how men who blighted lives of thousands evaded justice'.

The *Guardian* (14 November 2014, p. 17).

Foggo, D. 'Thalidomide victim Gary Skyner to go on hunger strike'.

The *Sunday Times* (13 September 2009).

Foggo, D. 'Fight for 'hidden victims' of baby drug'.

The *Sunday Times* (26 November 2011, p.12).

Handley, M. 'The day Bernard stopped laughing'.

The *Daily Post* (10 March 2000).

Hendry, A. 'Please don't buy them'.

The *Express* (29 February 2000, p.1).

Jack, A. 'Thalidomide – it's not over yet'.

The *Financial Times* (22 September 2007).

Newson, F. 'Gary has the last laugh'.

The *Liverpool Echo* (5 June 1997).

Scott, C. 'Thalidomide in Spain: the forgotten victims'.

The *Sunday Times Magazine* (3rd May 2015, pp. 12–19).

Teo, S.K., Stirling, D.I. & Zeldis, T.B., 'Thalidomide as a novel therapeutic agent: new uses for an old product.'

Abstract in *Drug Discovery Today*, (15 January 2015, vol. 10 (2), pp. 107–14).

Williamson, M., 'Frances Oldham Kelsey (obituary)'.

The *Independent* (17 August 2015).

Online References

BBC *Inside Out* London (18 April 2008, updated 28 October 2014). 'Thalidomide 50 years on'. http//:www.bbc.co.uk/insdeout/content/articles/2008/04/18/London (accessed 19 September 2015).

BBC News (7 July 2005). 'Compensation offer on

thalidomide'. http//:news.bbc.co.uk/1/hi/health/4658919/ stm (accessed 20 September 2015).

Bloxham, A. Telegraph News (14 January 2010). 'Thalidomide apology made official'. http//:www.telegraph.co.uk/news/ health/news/6988179 (accessed 20 September 2015).

Crawford, A. BBC News Magazine (24 July 2013). 'Brazil's new generation of thalidomide babies'. http//:www.bbc. co.uk/news/magazine/23418192 (accessed 19 September 2015).

Dove, F. BBC News Magazine (3 November 2011). 'What's happened to thalidomide babies?' http://www.bbc.co.uk/ news/magazine-15536544 (accessed 20 September 2015).

Haan, C. Leigh Day & Co. (August 2014). 'Forgotten thalidomide family admitted into the Thalidomide Trust.' http//leighday.co.uk/news/2014/August-2014 (accessed 20 September 2015).

Health in Wales (26 February 2010). '£1.9 million to improve care for thalidomide survivors in Wales'. https//:www. wales.nhs.uk/news/15660 (accessed 20 September 2015).

International Contergan Thalidomide Alliance (2014). 'Campaign information'. http//:ictacampaign.com/information.html#. vf8r79JViko (accessed 20 September 2015).

McMillan Cancer Support (4 January 2015). Lenalidamide (Revlamid). http://www.macmillan.org.uk/ Cancerinformation/Cancertreatment/Treatmenttypes/ Biologicaltherapies/Angiogenesisinhibitors/Lenalidomide. asp (accessed 21 September 2015).

National Cancer Institute (3 July 2013). 'FDA approval for thalidomide'. http//:www.cancer.gov/about-cancertreatment/drugs/FDA-thalidomide (accessed 20 September 2015).

Rowley, E. Sky News Online (23 October 2009). 'Thalidomide victim in hunger strike protest'. http//:news.sky.com/ story/733473 (accessed 19 September 2015).

State Claims Agency Ireland (April 2010.) 'Compensation for thalidomide survivors'. http://health.gov.ie/blog/publications/report-of-the-state-claims-agency-on-compensation-for-thalidomide-survivors/ (accessed 20 September 2015).

The Telegraph (1 September 2012). 'Grünenthal's apology in full'. http//:www.telegraph.co.uk/news/health/news9513858 (accessed 19 September 2015).

Thalidomide UK, (8.12.05) 'Historic agreement secures financial future for thalidomide survivors'. http//:www.thalidomideuk.com/#!diageo-covenant/ck2n (accessed 20 September 2015).

The Thalidomide Society, (2013) 'Compensation'. http://www.thalidomidesociety.org/compensation/ (accessed 20 September 2015).

The Thalidomide Trust, (undated), 'Patients know best'. http://web.patientsknowbest.com/thalidomide-trust.html (accessed 19 September 2015).

The Thalidomide Trust, 2015. 'The story of the Trust,' http//:www.thalidomidetrust.org (accessed 20 September 2015).

Wilkinson, E. (BBC News 23 December 2009). Thalidomide survivors to get £20 million'. http//:newsvote.bbc.co.uk/mpapps/pagetools/print/news.bbc.co.uk/1/hi/health/8428838.stm7ad=1 (accessed 20 September 2015).